DRAFTS 1–38, TOLL

Wesleyan Poetry

DRAFTS 1–38, TOLL

Rachel Blau DuPlessis

Wesleyan University Press
MIDDLETOWN, CONNECTICUT

Published by Wesleyan University Press, Middletown, CT 06459
Printed in the United States of America
5 4 3 2 1

Book design by Dean Bornstein

Library of Congress Cataloging-in-Publication Data

DuPlessis, Rachel Blau.
  Drafts 1–38, toll / Rachel Blau DuPlessis.
    p. cm. — (Wesleyan poetry)
  ISBN 0–8195–6484–2 (cloth : alk. paper) — ISBN 0–8195–6485–0
(pbk. : alk. paper)
  I. Title. II. Series.
  PS3554.U566 D68 2001
  811′.54—dc21

                                    2001003507

Cover photograph by Sandy Sorlein.

. . . the very word is like a bell

To toll . . .

> John Keats, "Ode to a Nightingale"

Feeling this, what should be the form
Which the ungainliness already suggested
Should take?

> Louis Zukofsky, "'Mantis': An Interpretation"

Contents

~~~~~~~~~~~~~~~~~~~~~~~~~~~~~~~~~~~~~

Acknowledgments

A 1990 Temple University Faculty Summer Grant, and a 1990 Commonwealth of Pennsylvania Council on the Arts Fellowship in Poetry, helped provide some of the time during which I composed this work. I also thank both The Fund for Poetry for a spirit-sustaining grant in December 1993 and my colleagues for awarding me the 1998–1999 Temple University Faculty Award for Creative Achievement. I owe a great acknowledgment to Suzanna Tamminen of Wesleyan University Press for the appearance of this work as a unit.

The Drafts in this book collect the series of autonomous, but interdependent canto-like poems on which I have been engaged since 1985. The pre-Drafts work, called "Writing" (1984–1985), and the first two Drafts were originally published in *Tabula Rosa* in 1987, *Drafts 3–14* were published in 1991, and *Drafts 15–XXX, The Fold* appeared in 1997, all from Potes & Poets Press. Hence I have a great indebtedness to Peter Ganick, the publisher of Potes & Poets. The French translation of several of the Drafts, called *Essais: Quatre Poèmes* appeared with Un Bureau sur l'Atlantique, Editions Créaphis in 1996, translated by Jean-Paul Auxeméry and the translation collective of Royaumont.

These poems initially appeared in the following journals and chapbooks. Some poems have been revised since their first publication:

"Draft 1: It" and "Draft 2: She," *Temblor* 5 (1987): 22–33.
"Draft 3: Of," *Sulfur* 20 (Fall 1987): 23–27.
"Draft 4: In," *Mandorla I*, 1 (May 1991): 64–68.
"Draft 5: Gap," *Conjunctions* 13 (Spring 1989): 40–44. "Trouée" [Draft 5: Gap], *Action Poétique* 136 (Automne 1994): 15–19 translated by Traduction Collective Royaumont. "Gap" was anthologized in *Moving Borders: Three Decades of Innovative Writing by Women*, ed. Mary Margaret Sloan. Jersey City: Talisman House Press, 1998: 336–341.

"Draft 6: Midrush," *Temblor* 7 (1988): 50–55. "Midrush" was anthologized in *Dwelling in Possibility: Women Poets and Critics on Poetry*, eds. Yopie Prins and Maeera Shreiber. Ithaca: Cornell University Press, 1997: 338–343.

"Draft 7: Me," *NOTVS* 4,1 (Spring 1989): 39–41; reprinted in *6ix* 1, 1 (Spring 1991): 4–6.

"Draft 8: The" and "Draft 9: Page" published as ABACUS 44 (1989); "Page" also appeared in *Conjunctions* 15 (1990): 243–247.

"Draft X: Letters" was published under the same title as a chapbook by Singing Horse Press, Philadelphia, 1991. In addition, some of the sections were also published in *Talisman* 4 (Spring 1990): 44; *Aerial*, and *The Women's Review of Books*, VIII, 10–11 (July 1991): 42. "T" was anthologized in *bite to eat place*, eds. Anne Walker and Andrea Adolph, Oakland: Redwood Coast Press, 1995: 79. "O" anthologized in *Moving Borders: Three Decades of Innovative Writing by Women*, ed. Mary Margaret Sloan, Jersey City, Talisman House, 1998: 335–336.

"Draft 11: Schwa," *Grand Street* 39 (1991): 26–33. "Schwa" was anthologized in *Onward: Contemporary Poetry and Poetics*, ed. Peter Baker, New York: Peter Lang Publishing, Inc., 1996: 143–162.

"Draft 12: Diasporas," *Sulfur* 29 (1991): 52–58. "Diasporas" was anthologized in *The Art of Practice: Forty-Five Contemporary Poets,* ed. Dennis Barone and Peter Ganick. Elmwood, CT: Potes & Poets Press, 1994: 19–25.

"Draft 13: Haibun," *Dark Ages Clasp the Daisy Root* #7 (April 1992): 39–44.

"Draft 14: Conjunctions," *TO:* 1, 1 (July 1992): 78–84. A version of this Draft was originally created for the "Poetry and Knowledge" panel (May 4, 1990) of St. Mark's Poetry Project, May 1990 Symposium,"Poetry for the Next Society: Assertions of Power."

"Draft 15: Little" (then numbered Draft 16), "Draft 16: Title" (then numbered Draft 15), "Draft 17: Unnamed," and "Draft 18: Traduction," *Sulfur* 32 (Spring 1993). "Little" was chosen for inclusion in *The Gertrude Stein Awards in Innovative North American Poetry: 1993–1994*, ed. Douglas

Messerli. Los Angeles: Sun and Moon Press, 1995: 90–93.

"Draft 19: Working Conditions," *Hot Bird Mfg* 11, number 14 (October 1993). It was reprinted in the Mexican journal *Mandorla 4: Mandorla: Nueva Escritura de las Américas/ New Writing from the Americas* (1995): 94–103.

"Draft 20: Incipit," *Parataxis: Modernism and Modern Writing* 6 (Spring/Summer 1994): 14–17.

"Draft 21: Cardinals," *Chelsea* 57 (Winter 1994): 82–88. A section also printed in *The World* #50 (New Writing from The Poetry Project), 1995: 103–105.

"Draft 22: Philadelphia Wireman," *Hambone* 12 (1995): 110–113.

"Draft 23: Findings," Sections 2–6, *Common Knowledge* 4, 3 (Winter 1995): 165–168. Sections 9–10, *The Capilano Review* Series 2: 17/18 (January 1996): 18–19. Sections 11–13 and 21, *Sulfur* 37 (Fall 1995): 125–128. Sections 16 and 17, *Lower Limit Speech: a newsletter in poetics* #11: 7–8. "From Draft 23: Findings" (sections 11–13 and 21). *The Gertrude Stein Awards in Innovative North American Poetry: 1995–1996*, ed. Douglas Messerli, Los Angeles: Sun & Moon Press, 1998.

"Draft 24: Gap," *Grand Street* 54 (Fall 1995): 172–176.

"Draft 25: Segno," *West Coast Line* 17 (Fall 1995): 122–125.

"Draft 26: M-m-ry," *The Iowa Review* 26, 2 (1996): 56–59. Special issue on North American Poetry.

from "Draft 27: Athwart," *Poetry New York* (1996): 73.

"Draft 29: Intellectual Autobiography," *Chain* 3 (Spring 1996): 58–65.

Sixty-six sections from "Draft 32: Renga." *Hambone* 14 (Fall 1998): 78–92.

Thirty-four sections from "Draft 32: Renga." *Conjunctions* (30th anniversary issue: Paper Airplane), (1998): 159–166.

Six sections from "Renga," then called "Draft 32: Renku," *American Poetry Review*'s *Philly Edition* (insert in *Philadelphia Weekly*), October 1, 1997: 14.

"Renga: Draft 32" was published under the same name as a chapbook by BeautifulSwimmer Press, Wayne Pa., 1998.

Sections from "Draft 33: Deixis." *Xcp* 4 (Cross-Cultural Poetics), 1999: 46–50. Sections in *kenning* (1999): 23–30 and in

Boxkite 3 (2001). This poem was delivered in earlier forms at the MLA, December 1997 and at the Postmodern Poetry Conference, University of Plymouth, Exmouth Branch, March 1998.

"Draft 34: Recto," *Gare du Nord* (1999): 8–9.

"Draft 36: Cento," *Chain* 5 (Summer 1998): 69–74.

"Draft 37: Praedelle," Number 41, Backwoods Broadsides Series, January 1999, n.p.

Sections from "Draft 38: Georgics and Shadow," *APR's Philly Edition* (1999): 24. The whole of "Draft 38" *Conjunctions* 35 (2000): 313–319.

Many thanks to the editors who have supported the publication of this work: J-P Auxeméry, Dennis Barone, Peter Baker, Robin Becker, Ray di Palma, Patrick Durgin, Clayton Eshleman, Edward Foster, Peter Ganick, Barbara Guest, the late Leland Hickman, Emmanuel Hocquard, Burt Kimmelman, Tony Lopez, Pattie McCarthy, Nathaniel Mackey, Douglas Messerli, Roy Miki, Drew Milne, Adalaide Morris, Bradford Morrow, Aldon Nielsen, Alice Notley, Mark Nowak, the late Douglas Oliver, Jena Osman, Gil Ott, Sylvester Pollet, Yopie Prins, Belle Randall, Bob Sherrin, Maeera Shreiber, Mary Margaret Sloan, Pat and Marla Smith, Rod Smith, Juliana Spahr, Jean Stein, James Taylor, Roberto Tejada, Eliot Weinberger for readings of "X," Kevin Varrone, and Lawrence Venuti. Thanks also to the gang of *6ix* (Alicia Askenase, Julia Blumenreich, Valerie Fox, Rina Terry, Heather Thomas, Phyllis Wat), and to the editors of *Philly Edition* (Ethel Rackin, Linh Dinh, Major Jackson). All puns, odd words, deliberate misspellings, neologisms, portmanteau terms, and plays at and with the letter are so intended by the author; these are not errors but rather errancy.

DRAFTS 1–38, TOLL

Draft 1: It

N.

   N.

           = =

and something spinning in the bushes   The past

             dismembered   sweetest

    dizzy chunk of song
                  one possible: there is a
in another   strange erosion and
dready fast flash   all the sugar is reconstituted:
             sunlight
silver backed   as 'stem': sugar as dirt.
light this
governed being: it?   that?

plunges into every object
a word and then some   chuck and
pwhee wee
half
tones
have tune's
heft.

          = =

I

One day lose him her
One day lose them

then it melts and dusts tomorrow too.
Me long   gone dissolutions   of
chucnk and humming a-
ddress it.
            have seen faces of limestone, stone cold piled
            unmortared, wandering, dividing the ranges; it
            lettered on green up hillside's social lining.
            divisions and elaborations of property, land-
            scape striated with historical sentence.
            have seen sheep, knolls, pebble turds in piles.
            A mark, a tuft, a makr   a/ a\
makes meaning it's
framed marks that make
meaning is, isn't
it?   Black

coding inside   A
white fold open   eye
open   a little
slip

                              = =

To what purpose reveal details of fleshy registers one
CAN have, blah blah   their charm? It's not
irony (really); it's awe.
They are what we are, we are
that,
that's it; it's only what we are,   we write our bodies
all and only what   begin space
(maybe)   by talking
the tizzy dizzy spin   at the window the
stars; a meaning's point   laid lines   weather
perfect,   the tunings talk
                                  in it;

two shadows blown

is one way of hinting it.

= =

It is not surprising that

It is not surprising,
that.

where in the placement of
saffron this is simple *you*
are listening *I* am alert
enough *she* is learning how to
talk *we* are reconstituted.

It
is not surprising That.

This is the spoilage of
presence   a condensation of

It's the little stuff that slips the wink   rot ick or
slides past phatic   split tingle
under all those sheets   "what
dog is woofing"   what shuttle
brights what warp?   WATER damage it really needs
replacement

Can I heed   you, it?

This line, scrawl of a bird line
tide line

= =

I feel the

The strange light scuds
jewels   to say
anything (it) must be   half-eaten apple

mistrusted.

    wedged under me in the car.
It must be loved like milk.

= =

3

(parole prevailing against long)
It, is so
long.

== ==

To reinvent "attention" is narrow tho tempting.
Doesn't get the folding.   I
is it

                          The
                                    generative
nor jargons in antiphon   mist
I always thought "antiphon" was the most

fat shadow.   beautiful word.   slight show.

                          A white house seems
                          to be a further
                          coagulation of mist
Lucite see-thru overlay, mark upon mark
glistening thru those microtimes of day. Stein in short was

No postcard poetry, a this a that like
a boat like a dog and not just any dog but   eliding
an over-eager retriever on waves   over
maybe like chickens bobbing.   the over.

== ==

CANO, can o,   yes   no
conno-
tations of impurities fill the fold.
Why that, or why
"sea blazed gold"
why
re-up anyway, to artifack
art pac, o me
o my.

4

= =

Nostalgia for a touch
resistant how
the language forms of sweetened
clouds   for fat and white   I love
you   Little whirlwinds of paper caught in the
clouds   cross-currents of systems (skyscraper wind
as clouds   tunnels, roads cut, built, then lined with
shadows creased in heaps and brights   delicate
                                        garbage, a land-
not literally thighs.   lessness even as we squat here so
                                on the land we are) the

                lyric?

= =

putt (pitting) the tiny word
litt
it
on stage in a "theatrical" space
a
space white and open a flat
spot a lite on
it   something
alight like wings.

Well now what's
to speak what is
to speak when that
Object (pronoun)
squeaks its little song its bright white
dear dead dark.

I hear. I do. YO! hear it
hear "it"? hand it into the wings.

dat dat dat

didn't want any beauty
tender
but

theater of the

        page   cream   space   peaks

           = =

      where in the space of particularity one passes
      beyond ego; where in the placement of saffron
MA ME I AM A WAKE a   and black tuft of heide, no
hoy ma milky-moo   hurt to the heath, not hold
bright boo.   the heart is empty being so
      full of a calmness marking minute practice.

           = =

Let silence
      in the form of words'
            in.   IT.

           = =

Some ART today:
a
mimetic use of mottled crepuscular marble to make a
pop ice cream
cone of,
vidi (!),
I saw—impossible
NOT to argue in light of it.
I'll make a representation
to you about it
later. After I end my song.

Shame is ordinary. Shamelessness
just a bit less. The real

interest is
limpidity,
power, the necessary

no and yes.   I wouldn't want to spread
Nos and Yeses incessant.   myself too pointedly.

= =

There's no way to read it?
one point is to achieve a social momentum of switched
referrents and (merry coral   white clover
ding ding ding) commentary in which what   he (you)
says or does must be read differently from what she
does or says whether he, you does it to her or them to
it (of whom?) she to it feels different (nights of Holly-
wood fascism) in an unsettling but not articulate way.
power power imbedded in, in its   (days of military realism)
place on the pronoun grid, cells squeak in protest "it's
just language" "we're just nature"

= =

TORN FROM (A PAGE)

a kind of orange it happens
a kind of orange
IT HAPPENS
rose rinse, vertical green.
Away anyway has shadow
"a typical Rachel shadow"
blue starts limb long and torso struggles
its window when all around there's not a single
wall, NO blockages
hardly stopped at all except by the pleasures
of color are you getting the picture
it hppns BLUEW one from the sequences of looming
comes   longing

= =

There's *no*; read *it*. Down
under where broach is, a
nuzzle a quick fat. It is the
"it" characteristic of everything.   Yes, read it!

   A narrative, a story, a plot, every word "a plot
   against the reader"; coagulations of it, rays
   pleased to be doing what they're doing not cynical yet

   and plenty spaces

= =

The struggle from whiteness
into whiteness
via black wit-

ness

I

ching.

= =

Overlope loop. Laugh language laugh.
Sandstone reach overload wrack
parabolic pools, warm line harken
shells   I

8

want to be *in* it, but it is not for
in it   it

is it.

Little girls little legs jump the wine dark line.

= =

No "books"   no ministers   no tow art

"no sandpoems"   build of it, not on it

it is sacred what you can do with it

the general aura of quest just as a baseline.

This silence awash with

bodies   flowered   aglow astripe to be

folded over signals.

Words' ribbon-wing hover, hovers, hovering.

Silence, silence, silence

was, this was, the implicit subject was

never foolhardy.

= =

Silences are the reaches of discourse

(rich incipit's big initials)

There is a yes and a no_{welled}^{walled} up

Sorrow? weeping yes and weeping no

it   is the definition of speaking;

gladness too is it, its weeping.

Silence is not the only subversion; it is.

The letters rise into a consuming which makes more

black fire flaming on white fire.

Fire fear (fears) fire. Scared is sacred.

Black arrow shot in blacker sleep

green word fold in greeny pock of folk

Speak, quiver, before your waves grow destitute

Dark feather dropped in foam of darker, antecedent sea.

May 1986–January 1987

Draft 2: She

The white one turns red they say
then peach to white   grass rich the edge-fold
space

slices of porcupine deep underground
and et that red-grained fat.

"I be good girl with my magic
markers."

(marks hands up red
makes henna dark touch)

Taboo thy ruses, moues and roses, shh.
Terra cotta, ochre smear of Provence

shadowy stains/stairs .

Ask for danger, say

"I want that danger."

∧ ∧

·

Who has

how images rise/rinse and erase how

can the rose
speak and how much

can you in fact stand that lobotomized
memory you have been washed up
into do you

NO?

Dear (name)
      I (morder)
          for departure's sake
further reaches.

The thin voice of the thin space.
Red red the rushes rise
down down by the salt tide veil, that
Love depicted as against itself:
small happy (guillotined) family unit
petal lashed to petal.

∧ ∧

 .

Families set like junket IN milky rooms'
schematic valleys—
V-shape of the young runnel;
rennet sweet-white jellies
over cascades of russet granite.

∧ ∧

 .

Lightly risen, of a plastic
pink too close, too
bare,
tho luminous Food one could imagine there
the Moone
when next I spy
retracts: a dime-sized toy-tied dish my moony

quest too dumb to ask a better/bitter question.

Still such catheter stuck there into my any fleck is
profligate.

∧ ∧

 .

Of suggestive twists, of wax rib

    jests
(twists)
    joists

stuffed by a potential crime,
do you read her as
"Mother"? "Woman"?

one-armed "Angel With A Lamp"?

  "Bandit
(Angel)
  "Badger

beam my way, beamy tinkling light; be me now
O Be Thou Me, sinuous one!

The piece, it's fleshy, picture perfect,
peachy... wax torqued up

to fill this unrelinquished peephole.
   fool

Luminosities   enormities of
key-shaped air in which she
flocks, twisted in brush,
sine curves verbatim.
A pubis allusive; the eye penises thru the keylock;
the eye is complicit and so is
     HUNGER

     NAUSEA

       hurl
for I am afraid to hole it   TOO MUCH
       hurt

not speak of hold me.

"I am your danger."
"I am your anger, ranger."
"I am your angel, dudgeon."

^ ^

.

Red orange with red veining
shading   raised

rib of same
color runs into large gold throat
suppressed heart, green.

Pale peach that by evening has a flush of pink

There is a pink rib goes
deep, up to the hilt,

rose heart, bound.
Between me? that?
heavy-eyed light gazing.

Daylilies open and drop
opal nenuphars of tears;

"I am your angle, stranger."

^ ^

.

Each word a cryptogram
Never too much:
in narrow, nah
in ride, rid
in courage, cor and rage

in flax phlox hemp feather, hook
garland   pull
a cryptic outline OF something
word shoal   staunched blood

food
stood at the edge of well-beloved veins

looking cock-eyed at all their deep,
at all their deep blue writing.

^ ^

.

Shadow under-word

lopes thru stands of wet papyrus—
microclimates for this ploy
versus that: rain warms here; wind twists there;
one family eats well, another eats each other.

House of the soul is filled with little
things, clay vessels, slipped and glazed
all smallness green leaf offering;
sweaty flower; baby loaf;
small as half an envelope which wads up tight
the poem's patchouli.

In shires, shrines:
you're going to have something
about aging teeth, you're going to have left
something half-chewed
in front of that house,

food on the plate of the moon?
mets sur l'assiette de la lune?

That hard to write
"the mother"? to get that
empty for that full

mouth(e)

her(e)

sh(e)?

^ ^
.

A borer, a beetle, an eater,
who will evaluate hunger?

Bowel, bowl, daughter
whosoever siphons undigested words
requires a wide tube.

^ ^

.

Dabbles the blankie down
din
do throw foo foo
noo
dles the arror
of eros the error of arrows
each little spoil and spill
all during pieces fly apart.
Splatting crumb bits there and there.
Feed 'n' wipe. Woo woo petunia
pie.
Hard
to get the fail of it,
large small specks each naming
yellow surface
green bites
Red elbow kicks an orange tangerine.

The time inside, makes tracks, seems a small
room lurches into the foreground, anger, throwing, some
dash, power swirls up against MErock, pick it UP,
Mommy me NEED
it a push a touch a
putsch pull a flailing kick a spool
for her who is and makes thread
"I"
The she that makes her her
The she that makes me SHE

^ ^

.

Practicing ferocity on your her self

You become the mother certainly a change.
             the monster   a chain.

16

Is this
foaling
failing the mother?
finding

^ ^

.

Top half poison   yellow light from above
ivy next half scritchings   blue light swells from earth
the garden red   bruising a frame

Digging, I sit on a flower.

Counting the steps of bright shadow, the pure pause, paces
clusters of ripe tones making up loud and then whispy forces
across one singular place saying no to itself with meditative
privation, yet unfixed, so spun out of, or of, being or
seeing. Which is not, but as it starts, starts a little
rivulet sound and voice, another, it fuses, pivots, a sigh
and sign; desire's design, blue transparencies rich for
thirst   listen, to listen is to drink
how can there be
another   cry: whom; one of another, who?
who cries? who listens?
hear here the liquid light
swirl and merge with drinking calls.
A sigh, a moan from what is waiting. Sweet sweet
sweet teas(e)
Another cry, a honey voice

Another
one.

^ ^

.

All told, a voluminous backdrop:
crevices of the night, 4:32 exactly
silver hush behind, curdling
a shaggy hurt bleat.
Eat that moon's sweet light.

17

Bird's blood is brown.
Her words, some said, they're just a
"bandaid on a mummy."

Wad reams of rems into mâché
my eyes chewing.
She screams unassimilable
first dreams.

Hold her unutterable

And press another quire of girl bound in, bond in, for pink.
Draw drafts of "milk" these words
are milk the point of this is
drink.

June 1986–January 1987

Draft 3: Of

Hinge-loss door, lack latch
ice-ribbed, straws, wad
T-top conglomerate, gritty glass
smash, street-glacier moraine. Pressed
particle board, its jujubes of shellack,
sweet sweet plastic lobbed hither
shredding rips, not too much shelter anyway,
guttering.

Little howling water marbles ice.
Peaked cans junk cubist shingles.
Trounce state cultivated motor auto.
Flop donut. Scat pretzel.
Uneased acceleration and diesel heavy
smoke shot straight rays
at an unseasoned toddler, some unformed
particles strain to come
"eye-shaped." The rest
could care less.
Everything
but weed slack's
loose with melted
writing.
Like one wrote IMPISM right on that rude wall.

Words come just like that, vision.
beak black bleak
cut back through arced site protocol,
member the day. Each micro-face splice gutted,
that
brekkkl they brekk the lyric ruck.

"don't call me a chef   honey
I'm a crook"

CUT

Skew. Gutter.
A woman scavaged food from that

cæsura. Which is
as traditional in this
setting as assigned
places: there's here, and there's there.
A there and a here (meditative
derivative) calls
"I" pivot, middle,
calls "I's" name,
sends "I" winding on site through all that middle
middle space so easily assize:
an assimilated viewer of
unfermented ground.

Would you note
the pretty poem
I might (therefore) of wrote?

It's this time-puzzled line-lumber fermenting place,
ice

of words, enormous slant, difficult OF.
Being. Junctures of saturation
beyond catalogue, yet catalogue HAS TO DO
do
syntax; how, why, being beyond me.
In the totality of its unstable relations
unstatable: the what.
This ice is treacherous.

Of is a voice and of is another, and there, here
of,
black and crest, the flair
"of things" in a langdscape.

Thick, this smashed bottle
green

on glaciated street ice, grey octopus.
Thicngs are the
juncted ponts.
Diecast power stick in your craw?
Well, fuck off.

A silent space (I
walk here) populous.
Possessed forsaken bridges, junk
things junked, a hinge from word to word a thingk
of what grammatical conjuncture can seem
adequate to "of"?

Another blizzard on our hands.
Avocado green, almond cream, blue heron, sunbeam
our choice
of colors   our choice of toppings   "rain" down

frozen treats snow pee snow white snow grey snow ice
snow peace snow gloom . . .

Amazing what a pack of fierceness
binds the backroads between tinker towns and makes
the garrulousness of these travellers virtuously
impenetrable.
We're all
(it seems) troubled by "them's"—
as far as it goes.

Hard to get home; but this is, this travelling
of
is
home.
The streets the malls a homey homeless home
ahung with things.

Micro things and macro things
flip back   "eat this"   "o boy"
in silence chomp your sugary
craw sand.

White snow-chemical for melting
purer than snow
beads the rows like
Hansel's bread. Some trail.
Some house. Some crumbs.
Protest, pivot, empty food-candy,
fatten you up child.
So thirsty
swallow wrong way a cherry
coke..Rub her
cough.
"Red spoil" backs up
the tongue wetting a small mouth'd paper – plastic sip.
Suffocate does it?
Discount!
The little MACS and diet YUMS and PUBS
we know.

Then talk to, about silence

in silence.

Cabin fever
in the grey
world.

Closer? farther?
To study and inhabit
(cars humping up the holding pit)
of, one foot after another, fueled and connected
(lapis and turquoise these are my birthrights)
to something inarticulable:
(rude grey nobs of street junk hinge the rough grey ice)
door after door of
of.

Quarrels, petitions, blanknesses, outrage,
collusions, buy-offs, conjunctions —
with something blown up

it is already here
the debris'

swift
exchange.

This gridlock of possessives
occupies the place
once held by distance.

February–July 1987; May 1991

Draft 4: In

Walks thru the daily
to write the dead

of living
in

every day, chopping
every day a changing, enlarge and isolate, o.

Herein
to dangle small specks over the cribside
surds   harmonics dang   odd
ratios   fishing an
anarchist page.

Oaten paper like bread,
ink of the living waves,
light billows in the grain,

Scritto. *scribe*. crotty
invents
fine fast lines and thick in-
ky turnings

fingerthin mountains
scroll
down to the narrow plain,
a pretty pass.

Creamy cup of tea
cool moon night
neighbor window light.
Unrolls accelerating
streaming

into the kine and pith
of basis.

How white "all color" the color
of luminous death
whose light
San Francisco   Provence   Paestum

is the color of my vivisection
in the world. The world!
the wheaty, milky world.

Whose years?
and what beg-
innings
articulate a blank blanked space, a dotted dotty line?

Just here . . . a draft, a stroke, a kind of fear.

The composted grids, earth lines
where
this hand shakes.
Late summer carnation pods dessicate in
spiky columns, blue grey green, each line is an
inter; there is no action, it is an inter,
(although it was genius to isolate
one action
and make it larger)
there is no story or poem
in.

Every day a little sweeping back, a little digging
out
in
a change
enlarging or diminishing can change.
Depends.

Inside the paper of the page
the iris watermark I suck.

A pen, a hand, an inching haibun,
riddle and edges:
tinted flings of ink wherein
inflection singing
bends time's
minute sounds.

In the backward and forward are
lower and higher
drawn out, drawn on, drawn in

a fine tip pen   a brush flick of
shimmer

amid which nuzzle worms and shaking dew.

Open eye buttabee.
Why the air so blue my honeyo?
Why incredulous by any change?
bud bud bud but bud bud
have turned (should some poem hesitate?)
lactate cherry words
milky spring
IN
to hunger of incipience, perpetual.

So one is finally of it and the "parts" and configuration are
no longer accessible. **Stars imperturbability
or matter's inside** Are dark. The mark is dark, the page
dark
is the first imagination of this drawing, this drafting,
these draughts. **Skims of language
scatter platters of plenty.** Patterns
that hunger. **A barque of silage through the sky is** as layers of
translucence, transparencies
on which words could be **feeding
the cow**

                    inside the ruminant middle.

read through the other, not so much over but the
simultaneous conflictual overloaded presences for which even
"palimpsest" is too structured a docket. Three dimensional
page, a page place or plage, a play space, a play splice
the flimsy drops of scrim through which they filter, shapes
and lights
                    I make the gesture
                        comes through me
                        A perfectly calm practice **it is this**
yet there is the tension of making a strange train. The run thru the
bi-lingual. Now a very long tunnel totally unexpected. Very dark,
and very long Entering under the whole structure of
transcendence **Long drawn black**
gold
bold in relation to nature. **fodder strokes**
And now there is no "in" in anything? any
deeper or more intimate **forage**, language
any   knowledge of the   **in** is some effect I
can no longer resist.   **Have no idea what** stop I am.
                            grassy drawing on white is
for me to show, to show me it, in. "The green horizon, early
winter dusk" is certainly pretty. I am not getting the force of it,
the rebuff,
this constant imperviousness laced with my pleasure.
Implacable

the world. The sorde serif I call myself. Because I am inside,
am a mite in the letter
a traveller thru **are, the senses of** dark holes tunneling grainy paper.
Gathering all because of being in it,
yet
I am getting the force of it, **in.**

August–December 1987; November 1988; May 1991

Draft 5: Gap

██████ photograph.
A man within a day
of dead

estranged in light, that
flat
flash struck,
half-holds his present

Strange

eyes whitened behind glass

Right on the edge.

              enamel a "modern" kind of minimal
              mural: indelible black rectangles;
              who coded the deletions,

lets a child
rip it open

. . .

              giving

              special numbers, offering a sheet of
              explanations to translate

"I guess I'll never see you again" I had almost said
              why the deletions had occurred.
"little child self"   but I meant "I guess I won't see
folds child soi(e)   it was careful and exacting work
pink silk, tan silk
stroked electricity.   many entirely black pages
              many black squares framed by

              grids of half-chucked writing

                           had been created
you for a while"
—dried—   by ███████████████████████
make golden "needles" engaged.

but I had spoken the truth
                    some pages you can't tell anything
hoarded. that aborted opening. one peers at those blackened.

an electric current   trying to read what cannot be read
not to touch
especially
with the "wet hands of tears."   "have been left out of"

2.

                    Black megaliths of memory
Are they too empty or too impacted, protected

Deciphering   "they evoke for me BODY" a dark
shimmer within a square   "activity of repressing
that might be   refabricating of making and
                                  losing" if this is memory

a rocking   I have an excellent memory.

of light
is it light? is it leaves? leaven? a place?
a dissolution opens a scattering of the lighter shadows
of shadow   but if it means actually remembering . . .

within darkness   the darker wall . . .

Every mark to touch a nerve
in a backwash
of silence   a cicadian roaring   "it is proper to go back

of silence: covers and articulates

the bugs crying to each other   to the shadows"

a close packed sound, their
impastos of fluctuating
distance.

The poem's poem   Black pages of gigantic books, tarred
a secret   glutinous with erasure as if
voice muttering porous you   asphalt food were spread
                                                    on burlap bread.

sprawled and fragrant

in a webbing of the gaps   Something read that cannot be
woven disclosure. . .   deciphered.

Low late pre-dawn freight
moans, or seems to
"J−w"
as it rushes the grade crossing

its track shining ahead
and away into unfillable

space.

                                        I said I had spoken the

On which plot

half wrapped in a sweaty sheet

a sheer drop:

one small point, one of the smallest,
if points had sizes,
yet such, that still
can barely imagine its densities and extensives

if all could be factored and scattered over the breadth
that is

and that
it is.

3.

Someone said this form: but where is it?
      one, start
      two, "the scattering"
      three, a "rush to finish"

even
metal link-
knot's unfathomable
ecliptic

swerving

stars—

Call that point "ʀ" on some
scroll of unrolling:
the there—   under a black square
that I "was once there"   cannot be read or found
all right

and in what language of uneasy rapture.

Grass stars, tree stars, dog stars
misty labyrinth

sores, spots, pocks, fats, jolts
teeming
constellations, and fecund milky spore
of galaxies on darkling sky

or pinked by the city
which dims the stars by local plethoras of light:

There,   with

little swinging words knots
bits   bugs
bite or shine

little guttering words . . .

August–September 1988

Draft 6: Midrush

Works
thru the dead to circle

the living flood-

flung expectations   lit wreathes,
and came to meet the cowering   wassail
pairs   doors and houses
in a tarred ark.   edged in blinking.

No one
could give particulars
enough
play, enough force
for what
claims

circles, pustules, chick-thick   circle garden overlooked
baby pox, MD sez boring   dying deeper down, flat
disease with flex enough to   even, from the last com-
twang a sour lyre   promises
"of days";   "of green";

pairing the letters
underneath
siting   citing
the writing under writing.

When the living began
to "labor" (as S. wrote,
rushed) "to die"

10 years work
10 years walk
foot fell into lemony simples

my heart at once in glee and grey
Bar David's star and Marry holly pricks
a day, all day, alway
had, has had had
unseasonable rip-tides
and easily washed away
the flexing thorns and toss amid which we;
shattered the nest to scree,

whereupon whatever thrifty
pots and bits, little
stuff, special mug,
had to be set rite, had to be
set. Assume it.
To paddle dog-wise
in a covenant of breaking—
I tell you!
Like always working against time.

Some flatten the paper
for next year.
Ark opened, the paired
zoo aired and marched.
The colors had been beautiful.
And we have gained more objects
whose provenance is tombs: lavish
pristine colors of the acrid lock.

Swirling marks and snags
low tidy times settle
clays, the pull sedentary.
Yet who will doubt the evidence
silted thru the claim-ragged dirt?

I labor because it was never
spoken and too much, or don't know
much. Or how.

Wraithes of poets, Oppen and oddly
Zukofsky
renew their open engagement with me
wreathing smoke-veils
my eyescreen tearing their insistent
opaque, startled
writing was speaking here was
saying words but,
befit a shady station,
sere swallowed up within the
mouths speaking
and all the words
dizzy with tears
passed again away.

"Where are they now
          dead people?"
"Nowhere."
          "But where
"ARE they?"

Human shards marked
markers ash the foiled
feathers of an eaten bird
maintain at the boundaries
of sense and tact
their dun features,
move
mostly much as did in life,
and away, blown
into the incomparable.

          What emptiness
          they cup for me
          from floods
          wherein they home?

"Death is the moment
when

what

has been given
away

must be reclaimed."

A clin-
ical rationalist
once he was dead
tempered his endless explanatory head
in wilds and wells of Hebrew prayer.

Walk thru the living
say the dead
our rustling voices
strain
more westerly words

BLOWN

when we have no more   back hosta pods
fluency   flat, black, glossy
cannot, as it turns   seeds
out   layered in the leafy mast,
form either fully   letter bits, the scattered
intelligible wonder or grief.   tabernacle.

It is they that speak
silt
we weep
silt
the flood-bound
written over and under with their
muddy marks

of writing under the writing.

Some epyllion—
pastoral, reclusive, elegiac: flooded
shards drifted up "forever"
thru the clay.
Always another little something—
a broken saucer flower fleck
unremarkable wedge, except its timing
working itself loose in the rain
thru the mum patch
and impatience
some glittery sharp a-flat the wet wide shade.

The house was built on a dump.

Or midrash—
overlayering stories so,
that calling out the ark, it's
Noah hails and harks
new name and number
for
what stinking fur and tuckered feather-fobs
did clamber forth
disoriented. Cramped. Half-dead.

Two names, four names
everything

paired
with words in secret twin
the dry the flooded
remark the same
thing the done
the continual

or unpaired, odd markèd dabs,
but somehow matched
together in their claims

walk thru the dead
to tell the living.

Dressed as a hunter
a robin
hood in tunic-top
of mother-lavish velvet
she talks swords,
greenling
"what are swords FOR?"
"for cutting people
like I cut the meat;
to try to hurt."

Rousing myself
to a cultural foray
attend, in Merz-y dote,
a chittering sonata.
Amid the *Europäische*
no sense glissades
repeats
this unmistakable refrain:
"rat-ta-tat-tat
bébé."

I will never survive
all this, narrowing skeptical
at straight arrow and oppositional
both. Where is my place?
The name is no.
Is name twin, double yolk,
no too? Is no plus no
a raggy margined yes?
Is no plus no a triangle
wedge of scribbled clay
worked thru claim-slid mud?
How even is with odd.

I get so homeless
mid-race, mill-race, mis-chance,
mezzo "cambio,"
it's lucky I've a house
grounded in this camouflaged locale.

I'm just trying to make
whatever rushed
arrangements
I can and can't
even hear
long distance

because nearer louder
"mommy don't go mommy don't go"
while I have to

work at understanding even
nominally
crossing out and re-
writing odd scraps
in the little ticket square, of days.

December 1987–January 1988

Draft 7: Me

Thru the sealed lid
"91st St."
wherein
mazed letters rem

was wrote, note, she

tolled sky writing:

and it was wide and it was
black—er—blank
a blue A
byss, ab
scess, am
bush,

em space.

—Sky writing—

White shifts, adjustable streaks, scatter
tracks, twigs fell fallen
slack on the asphalt;
the random drifts and drafts its
ens and ems.

Lucid cool green twi-day (say) a struggle
between different
voices competing   don't use that, meaning
that model   that word to identify
things that   this   isn't it   isn't my   voice

it?

A saturated brush it streaks and blots

a nursery easel struck
with spatter lines—what

speaks?

"me"—

her memoirs?

The big-mouth
bears came chasing me and made me
dash all dark—
far run of little me—and that started
some me screaming of
me, a tuneful tidal wave
of much engulfing light.

Do ray me
far so large.

The lines—of green, of pebbled loose—
a fall and scatter near, there mark their move.

Earth star
moon jelly
wobble in waters which
will sting, or sing
you, will

sing already full of voices—
polyphonous voy-
sizz—scissors that sharp
and flat line salt tide
signs:

many;

the sheer, sere
hunger of sight's all-stung

voy-elle. A voice says
"compete to identify." Worse than
jargon—unintelligible. Mental hunger.
"I can't believe my eating."

An old scribe's hieroglyphic-laden
stomacher on which one

Bright cold wide wet clear
writes feather hemp water pot combinations,
sits, placed my hands in beams of bright

tones, light
scales and sounds, sounding luminous
things:

Spoon face, lamp dot,
bread slice, old plate,
cold cup of creamy tea, the moon . . .

"You get to make a red line
on the door.
And then

God of The Death

just flew over their houses
and left them alone."

Listen! linen air
shrouds me in this baby swaddle
others are kind enough to see me running
as if for first-born and call me "her or me."

Dark wrapt. Enrapt,
the cricket breath of a small ark town,
a perch of stone, of pretty stone
the pretty pretty bird which sings a wet
wassail in morrow's dawn

thru naked bliss of space

lines

blow.

Really, could tell you all about me.

I line my eyes with blue
initiation. A bird-thought sits inside my throat.

Am, em a variable space
switched tracks, or dashing marks
which lie in wait
in every dark and light
that gleaming round or rounds this very spot.

Feather breath, I trill,
but sometimes stuck,
can't speak or spit what thrush I got.
So what, that's it, it's just like that.
Red sea, red sea, it covers me.

Spume ruffs
trace marks
no books
but dots and stripes on arcs;
plan
to withdraw my
candidacy, plan
to declare nothing.

And come, or comes, like the "Broadway I"

as it X's cross the knotted track and
boardwalk wedging shuttle cars marked "Grand Central":

And so I started putting writing
into my poems
and writing over and writing my poems
over—

grey-cream barley, dainty grain-slit eye—
tunnel-wet graffiti over soot patchouli—
cupped my hands, pink around light

rope spot box track signal,
treadmile walking, or riding, as I rode or write,
some sleep
or no—

and these were the fodder foods I offered them
from saffron rooms of light.

Of streams my eyes my hums their streaking lines
they

were all others, live and dead
others they brought
with them dashed into me—
some "me,"
that is, or
no me.

February–June 1988

Draft 8: The

sentences emerge inside sentences
inked on glass, pressured onto the paper
by hands.   A monoprint, grainy

Documentation is attended by a flat black wall
made of ink.
The tiniest point can be marked.

> dim and brilliant
> points, pinholes, dots
> of "the" like the stars

Days end, map bits, street locations,
"no continuing city" —
it's small-scale wandering here,
there,   precision of address. There's
> the dog, on the rug, quivering,
> her toes atwinkle with the dream,
> her falsetto "woof woof" tells
> she sees no telling what.

multiples that cannot (ever)
attach the points there are.

Toy-green plates
to feed the dead
little loaves, little flowers;
the "little" regions of fear
there, which   A squirrel throws down nuts
cannot even be   to make you go away, out of your yard,
> back to your house.

located, scanned
but evanesce.
Fall over dead
tired child.

"They hit   kick   throw stones
break things
run away   rage."

Sentences under
and over, marked,
as a blocked stage, with
tape for where to stand.

Odd books, broken bindings,
triangle flakes scatter out of the "sketches."
We were just going to talk.

A poem called "The" will always be a failure. It is the, the, the on a backdrop of enormous emptiness
that enraptures; just the sheer drop of it flaring against "clear sky in the desert" or "over a dark lake"

"Brilliant light brass
gold, with narrow scalloped, dark
margin."
Blueing tied in cheesecloth baglets
rinsed the water indigo.

can you imagine? It's impossible
even to understand the
littlest powder, or scaling, or why

the blueing (the coincidence of the name?
the "blau" "blue" "blew"?) is remembered
so clearly and bright.

What I saw or felt in sleeping who can say.
Ticketed for a "me" reel, flickering over incomprehensible zero space
as sonorous hoots of the freight train tossed and wept.
A sight, a sound, a thirsty mouth, a passing wave
4:32 exactly,
endlessly particular
and intent.

Something written on the side—
of what?
Strange changes of scale, and
Sentences inside
sentences, lines beside lines.
And here's a pink spot in the sky;
in the telescope like nothing.
Can't understand it, but just look—
a penny in some foreign money.
Mars.   Low.   And near.

Little precisions: solitaire
in a speeding car.

It's not a gloss either, in either of the senses of that word. Can't make head or tail of it.

Red and muttering, gnarled
whole thorns,
buds, ants at a picnic, fed like birds from her

ROUTE ITEM

Title: Drafts 1-38, toll / Rachel Blau DuPlessis.

Author: DuPlessis, Rachel Blau.

Call Number: 811.54 D936d

Enumeration:

Chronology:

Copy:

Item Barcode

3 2 7 1 1 0 0 0 5 4 5 3 6 2

Route To: CIRCULATION DESK
Columbia College Chicago Library
ILDS: COL
624 S. Michigan Avenue

Chicago
IL
60605
USA

thrown, she throws them
crumbs,
and struggles away deep in the
cross-hatched grass blades.

Every
day a chopping
a changing a swinging
back,
the blueing swirls an indigo
translucence.
The ants, the person X across a path.

The narrative of precise alignments cannot ever add up,
and to what? How anything ever holds together!
And the eye that makes it so. Which it might no longer.

Do "a work with many things at large."
Oil stains on the bread page,
a smell of acid paper and the flakes
snowing from "Un Coup De Dés,"

even the fact of a walk,
one "fact," one walk—
ovoid belly, open throated thrush—
generates multiples that cannot ever be
attached
or arrived at to greet. The monoprint
depicted *a* or *the*
down which the oily ink will pour.

And in that conjunction,
the dark of the moon.

Black coffee—tart, rewarmed, and acrid;
a cool cup of creamy tea;
two inch apart twin mysteries, a small
wedge SW arc, my blink
or blick of quadrant space
one silver blue, one golden red—
two planets very "close" together.
That is, as seen from here.

"Curved submarginal

silver-white spot band
basal silver-colored crescent."

"Below, deep, rich golden-orange
with sooty-colored overscaling."

These distances seem as
nothing
sometimes, and sometimes,
no proportion, without end.
A trestle terror on the dark train—
over what? held by what?

The indigo, dissolving, pools in time.
The planetary conjunction in some "now" now gone.
The paint upon glass,
pressed once into one paper
by one hand.
A bird in the brush; tree life; dog life; star life; my life.
An ant flicks into the sand-hole of its home.

> A blunt, baffled, continuous wonder.
> The poem boring, repetitive, and dull.

"The work is work, however,
and one is always in the middle of it.
For that reason, 'creation' is not creation"

but multiples that cannot
situate themselves as one
thing.
They were foreign
and distant when they were
near and violent.

"By now she knew almost nothing, no one,
but she knew the shape of the spoon.
She opened her mouth to be fed."

Day after day
with us the angels
grapple
in pinholes of light

plenitude and grief; of wordy words,
of wording words, I am
logy from touching the site.
"Let me go, for day is breaking"
I have forgotten what I am.

Sheens of A, luminosities of THE
crosslights and merging blind me
frozen on the thruway.

We were just
going to talk when I found
the sentence doubled, intercut, garbled out,
implausible, shadowed by its
struggling under sense.
Fought as equals
the attenuated shadows at dusk
the black of trees uncanny in the moon,
their deep inside-illuminated dark,
breath weeping harshly into breath
And doubled wrestling,
whitesmith, blacksmith,
And doppelgänger planets,
one blue, one red,
And in that conjunction
the moon, or no moon.

Silence, silence, silence
all unfinished
no detail selected, no pace
fabricated, no array of controlling disclosures.
This poem is flaw flaw flaw
for tetragrammaton awe
belies its formal tongue.
No worth. No form.

Just are. Or is. The the. A a. And what are
they? "What words they throw
away?"

September 1988-May 1989; June 1991

Draft 9: Page

> "Exegi monumentum aere perennius"
> Horace, *Odes*, III, xxx

1. Waste places from the very first.
Grubbed marginal plots,
where daisy aster, hairy petaled, was.
Saw sheaves of stirrers strewn by the loading dock.

Stepped and stepped
up the hill under the gate over the road through the field

into the reaches of some certain dead.
Spent mum
inside their rage

that every day decides it will not heal.
"This has been going on for years now."

Rage, range, some other "r" word, a re- or ru-
some word-hunger rampaging
its repression:

thus barely beginning, world, word, wood
would, as all varieties of clouds' lush chaos

BLEW.

2. She gave me loose crayonings, just
a few colored marks, and I was
frightened, first
folded my gift up.

"It looks terrible."
There is nerve involvement, codeine-sweetened pain,

negative dung. Without value.
In which becomes legible

a vacuum from the plethora of materials

and in this space a birth of enigma
to which one owes one's own enigma.

3. It was snow turning to rain, was soft sleet
sheets,
runnels of grey air, was melting on the asphalt, was nothing
to last?

All the words of light,
light among ancient peoples, navigators,
hidden.

Irretrievable estrangements and
unanswerable despair primed
thick-weave canvases which I stretched here.
It was almost too much, it was almost
smothered.

4. For the canvases already primed with words
were to take more.
And the line-streaked white
wobbled

perennially ready
to hold another streak or counter-score.

Eggshell colorings when cracked
show turquoise bleeds
upon the over-boiled white.

Softly silted S's silver water
silk the misted phosphorescent ground
beyond the river's main meander.

A space for deep wake

(screamed "something wet is chasing me"
or "there are worms in my bed") then
the deep wake, passing.

5. Dawn white
Sunset green

Muddy turgid dirt-like clouds
rainbow arch, and driving madly toward it

rows of makirs
litanies of dead, and dead too young

sequences
interruptions

"making light do what I want"
"weaving webs and webs of silver"

whose very whiteness may be thought too blank
to "tell the white marks from the black."

Apprenticed to it
tripping, my nose down, one corner of an iris, a stick,

light making me do what it wants
and it wants me to weep.

The luminous sheet, the open space, is living air and bright;
or dead, a waiting white like night.

6. What do you want? Is the poem a pony?
You want it to be "noble"
and "stronger than bronze."

You talk of funerals.
I have put a half-sprig
on a coffin above what once had soon before
a face. But was no more.

The poem immortal? You guarantee?

These page-space presences the
negativity
of written words; "parsley" or "bronze," are
airy

as if they turned beyond dimension
and cast the shadows
of what nameless void, whatever voiceless space collected
behind,
and beyond.

Dangerous their generosity
coupled with that shadowy randomness.

7. I crack the spine
of the book, split its muslin glue,
chip the endpapers in a ragged rip.
Inside, folds
and mats of list
camouflage as lines.

It's hiding its impulse even from itself.
Does it want to speak?
Does it want to weep?

Mist. It's four. Rigid without sleep.
"To know what my motives are . . ."
(unfinished)

8. Line marks names
wavy registers,
a note with folds on the edge of a used sheet
a note with staples and tape
crumpled paper, pencil smudges half illegible
"isolate flakes" hybrid, subversive, inchoate.

The writing on the open page

the underside of itself
as if the underside made words
and, when the busy ripples on the surface stilled,
one saw that other taking shape:

the abstract rush of untranslated words

the space a presence possessed by other spaces

white trace
blank trance
whisper hold.

9. Being the thing that light comes round, it comes to know
light.

Black, and black and white;
yes, and no, and yes and no;
being and not:
the flicker over space—rectangle, letter line,
spatter marks, irregular alphabet, rath and late;
a scrape, a set of incisions, a score in air:
for various work
has been done in and over this place

various works or workings, works
by,
of,
different hands

hand-space tracks
trek lines

(a trace of spotted light
gleams around the tricky edge of substance . . .)

February–May 1989

Draft X: Letters

> This is the alphabet qwertyuiopae[s]dfghjklzxcvbnm.
> The extraordinary thing is that no one has yet taken
> the trouble to write it out fully. And what is a beauti-
> ful woman?
>
> William Carlos Williams,
> *A Novelette* (1932).

Q.

I don't know.

What is "natural"
for letters, bud-feathers,
small bumps clumped along my twig.
"Quarry?"
Not an easy question.

Speechless
between each word: years
shown, shone
as quads, months queue;
lead-based slugs line
quoin wedged, double-tied in their chase
by a printer's master knot.

Spaces—
this very minute. Dazed

quagmire.

Of time.

In fact, stuck.
Woman? Letters?
Struck.

They fell from the chase
astonished,
touched to the quick.

W.

Dear X,

                         Dear who?

Waking at night
with   what about?
penetrating rain, rain
awash thru the screen
wetting
                    She had failed
a grid-wire window-net.
Telling
time is it like reading:
            to tell herself what she wanted.

these silver water particles,
shimmering square bubbles,
extend their gridded meniscuses into a space
where   Hard, even
even the smallest
are, or R   to have the stomach for it.
mystery
dank clouds, dirt path, back pack, dead leaf—
this roving, this woven
red leaf, crumpled wrapper, waste water, weeping wound—
whatever
wedges up an intersect,
weights
this or any temporary X.

E.

In eating, I skim the sticky flats called
"Plenty." It is a strange site.

Have some! can offer
nice engineering
in pretty packages of crackling;
in quaffs of flavored water
a strange, estranged air.

What is enough?
If I eat for the hungry, there are many.
If I buy the coupon'd food,
I crunch sugar and pee salt.

Everything o so "good" and E-Z

to eat for the dead, for the dying,
to keep them in my belly, fetally, or fecally.

R.

Arrived
So soon!
      In the lull then
R
Runs the road down hill.   rain, rain and space, and rain
       swooning, turgid day

She scrolls, runs after unrolling
      wet sweet grass in the grips
now it's all downhill, and uphill, too,
it's all uphill,   of
running up river and down river.
Can't remember   this
no matter what.   flooding.

O no matter what, I say.

Pigments

So I say,   "R"

because it figures, but hard to figure it,

it's   rubbed, scrubbed, marked and

repressed.   erased.

T.

The tea cup in the soft lamp light
travels its little tea breath and milky waves,
its train of time, sentimentally.

I'm thirsty. And it was a question.

 And something   To which the answer is:
                                        there is no "beauty."

            ties
            tries   it.
            tires

                                I can't get myself
Faced   *the simplest things*
                                make yourself a cup of tea
with the tarballs   *somehow*
                                I have to get thru this I cringe
                                every day I cringe
                                It's like living in a tomb.

officials are taking a wait and see
attitude.

Y.

Yet every word is a plot:
so story, a story,
why not tell a story, travelling yare and tidy.

                                        Two years or whatever
                                             to the day
                                        by some coincidence.
                                             There's mesh netting
                                             yoked to the cliffs,

                                             because
                                             unstable rocks

a "yolk-yellow" melon,
a diagram and not a poem
a diagram and not a painting:
no need to "fill in" all the color.   present a danger.

Your irony about a voice lavishly remembering.
Because you can't.

U.

        Under these urgent, repetitious refusals
        are grids
        extending
        an unconscionable
        breadth.
        Can never say enough

                (unspeakable)

        brown crust spurt:
        sparrow upstart in a bush,

        whose eager range-drenched beak
                (peep peep)
        thru unguent amber, calls,
        and resonates
        with undertexts.

        Beads of amber,
                (peep)

some contain trapped creepers,
are loosely strung upon undulations of umber.

I.

Lavish but inadequate.
Insufficient.
"I"
inside the fabled site
X ist
X'd out.

Is it inexcusable
to write an elegy for "I"?

"I have nothing to say,
only to show.

I will not present anything
of value.

But the debris! the refuse!"

O.

Overwhelming.

Stuck   They try to tell you
two owls hooting   The feel of dying.
thru and thru
the domèd cupola of night.

I lose my breath.

water-mouths
Oak
tassel-flowers   *Weighing my options.*

fall.
So much for fall, for spring,   *I lose my breath*
so much fell, outside in and inside out

And if it falls from the sky   *someone must*
with its ossuary payload,   *stay here.*
its slivers of the invisible,
its X,
malpliklarigo (to fall, as of snow, Esperanto)—

the foot, pan, rope, loaf,
and wick of twisted flax
oat toast
                    "The orphic hope"
                                for a singing stone
the wane and wax of
other alphabets,
primers
of Adams and of Kings,

their one word
(Xantippe or Xenophon)
stand-ins for narratives of X,

and me at my hieroglyphic   Or for orphic ears, to hear,
Mac, as high   or orphic, orphaned mouths,
toned as a Xerox,   "oh oh"

            A well with clefts, letters as stones.

P.

                Pretty doll plates
                of the dead

                red clay, green glaze
                little pips, gifts.

                I am hungry for the food
                left for the dead.

                But I know I should not eat it.

63

A.

Always apples
are (R)
first:
red planes, yellow planes,
green squares, the most provocative
modeling   Welcome to Aberdeen.
set and round. Piled on a plate.
Articulated by bunting.   Proud to be American.
Apples, A
premier symbol
on the table —
Au and O and I   No Flag Burners Allowed.
Cu and C, K and Ca —
of elements.

A
solid type of art.

S.

Especially sediments of unfinished
stories, eroded stories   she states what she has eaten
                                           says
                                           can scarcely swallow

          "stickers stamps bus transfers postmarks
          clippings paper textures phrases letters"
          voluminous overlays carried by valise
          "a more spindly and papery space"
                    Imagine a work
                carries   on
            scissors too, plain paper   transparencies of plastic
sheet over sheet   sheet over sheet, scrim light
and glue   sifting words' densities: that slide
in the suitcase   over the others, network by network,
                                           that darken

might fall open, might   blackletter solid, thickletter solid
spill at the Gare du Nord   thru which

words: piled into strata
swirled indicators fallen askew, faulted, syncline
scribble scrabble
overwritten, no one way of
ascertaining   something
        and everything
is like this, simultaneous,
readable in some parts and sometimes in
other parts, or in the same parts, un-

D.

Towers of tires the dead dog was
chained there to guard,
dead bitch skeletal
but still sleek, her beautiful fur,
at the foot of the rubbish heap,
starved.
Long starved.
Her master elsewhere.

The dead are the food
        left for us,
                but don't be greedy.

The door cut her foot.   *It's as if doors are closing.*

F.

Such newspapers as blow across the field
sucking the trash news against the fence

        Antenna Sales and Install
        Finance Plan Percent
        Ho Maid Bakery Products

The military
flew in to dine
at Mt. Rainier Lodge
by helicopter.
Fine use of equip.
Show how something done.

Five pair, then five more pair,
take more, another color.

In the morning,
              the news

On the train,
              the news

What has
              happened, has been done, was
              forged and fulsome
              in my sullen name.

I am poisoned
              thru my ear.

The players
              poured it there.

G.

A genre:

              Ballet blanc:
"The most poetical subject   gauze, tulle,
is the death of a beautiful woman"   gossamer
the floating wedge upside down   golems of passion.
that works by electricity.
        Swans grouped in a graceful, nervous gaggle.
How about that!
        "Je
        ate un autre," all right.

But if "Elle
suis un autre"
it seems to be she
follows another or copies another.

Gender

headlight eyes

adieu.

"There's a company where they've gone
beyond gender.
If they wear dresses
everyone wears dresses
—the men wear dresses."

Yea, I will bud out, butt out, yea I will grow
my own green garb, from my own fat self,
and girlie pink socks, toe hole in the sneaks.
Awash
in jumping
I will catch him and her
I will catch and caught whomever
leaps into my flying arms and legs
and dance.

H.

No more frames—   *My hair, it has come out*
no nothing   *it had to, and the heat,*
more than: X marks, like the "yellow spot" in the retina
"my spirit imbedded in glitter"   *I have to wear a hat*
I need the guide to cross-hatching.   *or a scarf, but the heat, it's*
It's horrible,
it gladdens the heart, everything is happening
Do you have one?   *very hard*
                                      to wear a scarf in the heat.
at the same time.

J.

Plague of the first borns
joy-riding through cocaine.   The J of "jour"
Junk subdued, junk exaggerated: truck backs graffito'd,
wire rolls, stereo sets wiring and micro chips matting or "journal"
strung out of cars as discards, rainbow wads of wire
by the jerk-offs.   the thinnest shred of paper!
So much for sentences.   So much for painting.

K.

Try Esperanto.
Try some mittel-Europäische cooked-up koiné.
The sign indicating "rough air" what
they no longer call "turbulence," too
unsettling
the coincidence to trance
to translate Eng. to Esp. and having
all the whirrs the words come out with initial
K's.
Blow down and powder,
diasporas of letters,
the brown rain of stuff
oak tassel-flowers,
kverkoa kvastoj-floroj,
brown   *I have*
strings of quipu   *no choice.*
spring
rosaries of pollen.

L.

It was lost. Memory lost.
"So much time spent looking down the track."
The el dislodges at 242nd St. terminus
lumbers to 238th.

"Let me out of here!" I remember
late   One day they will cull dictionaries
                                       looking for flowers pressed long
                                       ago by sentimental ladies, hoping
                                       among them
                                       for such seeds as would assist
                                       to restart species.
gestures of leaving.
Hard to know which

                        The scale   the land   the rocks   the riches
                              the places   unspeakable.
                        The whole continent driven over a cliff.

memory lost? memory compressed? a dead letter.

Or it was not lost, milky mist moving through the valley
layering pearl cloud, it
was that "memory" was not only "mine"

so it lacerated in ways akin
to clearcut overlogged landscapes
dotted with foxgloves and even-sheared stumps.
And what I am mourning is not "no memory."

Z.

            This letter shored
            a book of blackened facts;
            it faxed the facts and sent them
            to itself,
            it turned its very pages black.

            Dark water Zee rose up to cover them.

            Hardly could it be read, even by holding books
            to the light,
            so thick with inky figures it meant
            zero.

Figure after figure
in a row   z after z
It meant sleep.

Sleep in your villages
of stone, and little towns of styrofoam.

X.

"So what does 1 + 1 equal?"

"One!"

Index to it:
        apples: of Demuth, with bananas of
            of Vlaminck, saturnine quality of
            of Cezanne, impossible to "describe"
        attention, kinds of; awe; ambush.
        Blow, the recurrence of
        Cancer, the hungry recurrence of
        See also debris.
        Daisies: of Demuth, with tomatoes of
        Emptiness
        frame
        grids for the
        hunger of
        It, as a shifter, its galaxies,
        and junctures
        kited together like odd fruit and crockery
        in still lives. Apprenticed to the Mastery of Textures.
        Sez Letters! I don't know why
        ex-margins' negativities are so sculptural.
        Nor what multiple factors
        are at issue.
        Nor if Many (if arranged well) equals One.
            the little pot of,
            the oatmeal of,
            the scale of.

Page, as pink. Or black.
Quire, one-twentieth of a ream.
Poem: bare ruined quire.
Rachel, the pinkish color of a powder.
Silence.
Triangle leap. Solomon's seal.
Totem memoranda: the
Unutterable is or are
Voluminous.
Woman, as a well-inked
    letterpress. Kohl round her eye;
    she splots on the page as she falls.
X, it marks the spot. It hits the spot.
And marks taboo, and intersect.

Why, as *why*, spoken by the dead.
And dizzying, dismembered zed.

C.

See the staining color, strange cakey streaks, ochre and ombre
that countersink the flux.

Colors create
shadow, they have dimension, they can scale
horizontal connectives, like clefs.

> *I feel a lot of changes*
> *going on.*
>
> *I have no choice.*
>
> *It is disaster faster*
> *than I'm prepared for.*

Chrysanthemums violets lobelia orchid
dragons, coral and fire, cobalt, cerulean,
carbon, cardinal, carrot, celadon. These colors are lettered,
heightened in intensity by celestial names.

And in the University Museum, a
Chinese bowl shines, quivers, overglazed; it is slathered with
chicken-schmaltz yellow,
a bowl the sheen of childhood fat.

Curator, did
you cut the child's cord with crystal?

I dreamt of doing CPR
into the contraband rictus of the dead.

V.

Vermilion, muttering, it was
that the voyage also framed the vulva,
that the day vexed it, vibrant and articulated.
It had black velvet strings drawn tight
bound like the piping around upholstery
knots tied to hold forward or down
aglow astripe!   All seasons. Her lymph gland
                              swollen like a volleyball "White
                    territory?" not white it has a verdigris
                    black long screen a square of blackened
                    import it
                    has a purple mottle wounded friction
                         has
                              a white as green as bluish gripping grey
                              as the skin of a strange valediction.

B.

Black nettles soft redfold flower
blazes of polychrome
Can I say something to console you   Body leased
while trying (one-handed) to undo
the binary?   yet one's only boundary.
The room is dim   Tenacious tenant

a little tush is raised.   evicted.
Four windows
a full room
a touch half-pulled
the clear emptiness brimming silver light.

                    Three robin's eggs,
                    blue and unbroken,
                    lay in their crisp blue nest.

          Cielito. My little sky.

                              I will be ashes
                              blew
                              out on the street
                              blowing thru the night.

N.

N negative plus N positive   "Needless to say,
equals   no amateur
zero, but it isn't   should ever attempt to excavate
as if nothing   a prehistoric burial mound."
had happened
is it?

M.

    "Since, as we have already said,
    everything in the experience is in motion,"
    No memory   Earth mounds
                              ruined by road cuts.
    How can time be made demonstrable except by its debris?

                    For X. Of X.
                    I. M. X.

Coda:

Now, for a metaphor,
it could be a black page
or a white page,
or a radiation treatment of the page so that the words
have fallen out

like hair.

And memory, they say, is the "mother" of the muses.
And mother is the instruction not to speak,
to speak partly, to speak euphemisms,
or mesmerizing euhemerisms, to
speak half-deaf to the undertext, to never notice
wantings,
to swallow mourning
to swallow the burning over and over so
that tubes and lobes are scarred with
stig-matter.

Which in order to set forth
must be scattered
must be shattered
smashed against a wall, a door,
thrown against the inoperable sealed-up exit.

January 1989–May 1990

I. M. E.W.B.
June 19, 1914–May 3, 1990

Draft 11: Schwa

The "unsaid" is a shifting boundary
resisting even itself.
Something, the half-sayable,
goes speechless. Or it can't

and Inbetween

              what is, and
              that it is,

is ə Inside

. . . . . . an offhand
sound, a howe or swallowed
shallow. Sayable Sign
of the un-.

. . . .

Not the exotic
that is strange but this *strange* puzzle
coil cup "here" where time goes forward

              floats by
              boundaries

a memory *of half*
sayable vague,
and textured *what*
. . . . . . *and that it is*
rose or knit or mother-of-pearl
goes speechless
 marks the child *makes* letters,
a signature graffiti, film stills,
saffron light on a west soffit, *Inside.*

And Inbetween

. . . .

lost objects, a tiny doll
and her SWEE-TOUCH-NEE
tin tea trunk of frills.

. . . .

There was a set of girl hankies, saying Monday, Tuesday,

it

the glimmers over 7 new days.

Wednesday, veiled,
those patches of old ice
swampy around tree roots,
low, soupy grey now
so that a great mist covers what was
dirty embankments,
clouds glowering in the nooks of soft valleys
as I rode or ride
so away I do not recognize the vacuum
. . . .
walls of dreams
. . . .

A Thursday, some small good girl
speechless
twirls her plaid umbrella, Friday,
the details.
Struggle tableau:
squeezer-siphons suction out the mucousy sinuses.
Framed from the outside, the flailing
careens thru schwa time
a darter from the murk of silence.

                    Are lost. Most.
                    Things of which.

Old familiars, hook toes in amber.
"as still aware as"
Bits matching or unmatched
"gurnish helfin." Can't helf or heft
can't scarcely help
the looming empty weight of emptied time.
Carry an eviscerated bird.
The rubber chicken of a melted past.
Whose kosher yellow feet cut off
stuff up the vacant cavity.

. . . .

Lunchbox thermos
shatters slivering into

All little tiny "it's" and "its"; there was
a shifting boundary *that is strange*
Open the drawer *speechless* Of all the lost things
never reseen
hardly bearable never
recoverable, here is something!
An orange blotter! on which brighten
cough syrup bottle- and bird- profiles
edged with a tiny ruler.
WAMPOLE'S CREO-TERPIN compound,
Conjunctures detailed and lavish, Mott Avenue,
Far Rockaway, some of the ten birds
(nested, pecking, chirping, or in flight)
became, in the four decades interim,
endangered.
Other conjunctures blank. Years
this incredible life in time
"simply" erased.
yet day by day the bits and crumbs
wiped up *by what invisible vectors*
lost *not lost; half lost,* and lost.
A random swirling pulse of bronzed leaves
breath of a wind intense and subsiding, so

some *falling* here, some over there. . . . . .
like Betelgeuse and Rigel, 200 million,
where the light lands
whose faded thread chance calls
the pulse more powerful more bright
its factors more unfathomable
than any thing we know.
And we know nothing.

Yet the blue twisted inner
tinkle of milk poured out the broken thermos
in which mirror-like glass bits splintered. . . . . .

    YET WHAT?
    Is this

rubble accountable? Half-memories, memories half
empty, schwas of memory,
Things, half Things, Things'

effacement. Shadow somber lesions
slopped and filled by creamy prime, so that
almost, they are drawn back
to the stretched silence of canvas.

. . . .

Made in China,
marked down sweater
now marked down half again
to really cheap:
that I,
whatever that is,
can,
without particular investment in it,
stand in the mall,
drawn and quartered like a heifer
trying this
thing in which filiations

(geopolitical, material, and narrative)
thread, and are stored.
Signs readable, but also embarrassing.
"It's so now." Just
a Knitting whose rich patterns
shuttled thru dark labyrinths
"punch up your Look."

How many miles
have its bumpy acrylics travelled
to have come thus far,
to Springfield Mall,
adrift from its pence-paid maker. . . . . .
The weave of its wefters, its shunters, its buyers,
its filmy yarns' dictation and direction

                    Who can
                    must Credit.

And the bright tags and the price codes are tacked in plastic
string,
and anchor it

a sound halfway between articulation and disappearance
a sound falling out
or beginning to fall out,
voiced, but seemingly voiceless.

. . . .

Unheard vocalics taken for granted
are making, are mocking up
words, that
no one can put their finger on, yes
abrim with scrambled schwas
and unfathomable glissades.

Just as a febrile distracted

ichneumon bug, the leggy one,
wavers shadowy from corner to corner,
flies panicked, and climbs treadmills of wall,

this loss seems irrevocable.
I quiver in my pinhole time
where bits of voice are buried
in broken, unrecoverable objects,
the flowered butter dish, a-smash
Trip films torn from a stolen camera, and dumped,
bits and turns, the buried sounds of stifled voicing.
And were I to cry that out, who'd want to hear me do it?

        Gap and glut
        "most people"

remains between the two
"unwritten."

And cried out
who would bother to listen
among those frantically fluttering angles?
. . . .

        Bunched up.
        If only.

Thus, travelling hungry, I lost my sense of direction,
with "metamorphosis"
and "petrified human desire"
my dearest companions.

                      June–November 1990

Draft 12: Diasporas

Thru the rusty furze, thru the misted light,
thru the hungry books
words
related to the torn debris
lightly fall,
brush
the stumbled walker
who enters scenes of scattering by the gate of loss.

Wordlessness   whirlwinds   words
at that limen, articulating multiples
that cannot even be attached or
arrived at to greet, so foreign and distant, and
so near and constant,
the sets were experienced as one confusion.

These spaces of dispersion
are marked with bourns
which disappear amid the fields of scree
as stones.
So gifts are swallowed up by gifts.
Even erasure is erased.
In this, what residue remains?

The green horizon, winter dusk,
curbs, ground-down dabs,
sleek styrofoam weathered into gritty pebbling,
food pressed face down on the asphalt
scattered
          thru the flicker-ridden labyrinth,

                    here

                    we are,

gripping frayed ends of the yarn together,
bull-face and seeker.

This small evidence of hope, that our flawed light

MEASURES THE HEADLINES

warily
point for point.

'Twas the new year cold,
and the old year done.
Hung a full moon
twice that 31st.
It rose in the dark,
and it rose at the dawn.

Introducing the "J" of jour, the our of hour,
versus "A": flat, primary, simple.
First it's J.
Then it's A,

parry and grapple, sleek and troubled,
leg over leg on the shimmering tarmac.
Advantage agnostic.

Happens
your yeasty jousters
are oddly,

like Ques. and Ans.,
odic and oracular,
joy and anger,
just evenly matched.

Matted mists rise
from felled leaves
after the whirlwind.

Melted mists
mishegoss and worse,
Names that cannot rise.

Names wedged in cardboard huts from
      major appliances.
           Photocopying

city by city;
      stacks on automatic feed, little
          rustlings over vents,

mechanisms under glass,
      darkly you thought
          THAT was a what?

an empty carton? THIS simply
      rags, drain-plugs, trash
          rolled up in bags by the Department

of the Treasury, askew
      and stinking. But look:
          what is and that it is.

      On the pivot
      of a vast immired time
      the little fizzle of firecrackers
      went pop-pop in the humid silence,
      the irradiant bleakness
      of this midnight turn. Why it's "already"

1991

one more throb of pops down wicks flung into the distance
      and all around a void of open time
      to the right of us, to the left of us.

          And want to rise up, compelled
      to change the order of events,   to overturn

priorities and registers. Own up
powers dominating an unseen. They
solid for war: And drag to camp that Trojan
Horse,   the surgical
metaphor. Of course, modernized,
administering anaesthesia highs. But
who was the patient "etherized"?
We profiteering, prophesying, sighing.
The center, an abyss   The A repeated useless over
and over   lolling doped
uh uh uh uh uh uh uh uh uh uh ayh ayh
turning to I I I I aye aye aye aye ai ai ai ai
scattered by one, one, one   waste pretense. It was the dust rising
and falling that formed the holden
source of all this "dreath."
It was solid blackness up from the dis(re)membered
ordures and ordeals.
It was children once again to be issued bumbled stumps for feet.

My m-m-ry looked back and turned to salt.
A glistening dolmen.
Does it want to weep?

"It" doesn't choose
"It" is chosen
by the frozen one-way track
of time

Implacable

(Light!
"opening" birds
"lofting, spinning"
transcendent flocks
flecking the wide "horizon"—signs
of a poet,
or for one.

Why not car roof snow slid soft,

and refroze drip-marked over the windshield?

Why not furtive copies, ripping off
the part-time joblet,

with one long hair
fallen onto the glass screen, recurring
on all her X——xes, twisting at random,
circling words.

Dingedicht, Dongedacht, Dingedicht, Dongedacht)

And into the valley of death
I or J wrestled
pulled apart at the jointure or juncture.
The little rocks and bumps
were welded together with blood, and blood
filled the streams, which were called "runs," and
misty blood evaporated in the hollows.
Such a tiny set of hedgerows over which the soldiers fling
and were flung.
Cost it out.
The deep hung crevasses of shape and meaning
make
just a flicker over ever-whispering space.

"Then" I felt the dead, returned as deer, sidle
silently in the night to the block of white,
rub and lick

mutter in the various
clotted tones of
their living voices

one word:
creole of creoles.
The rest blown away

Into the incomparable.

<pre>
                     Struggling with
Unfed. Thug. Bread.   ashes wet
Flagged pilings. Blood maimed.   ashen face
Flayed pages. Manna and matter   in the drear station

                  and historical dread.
</pre>

So that the first digits of my MAC card are exactly the number of
civilians killed at My Lai or Mylae, alongside the final digit, which
is the number of persons in my family, allowing, or not, for the
ambiguities of reporting, lies, cover-ups, disinformation, disingen-
uous spokespersons—so often now women—, and who or what
one is counting; also whether one numbers the dead and the liv-
ing, or only the dead, or only the living, on either the "historical
plane" or the "personal." Or only numbs the living. So that there
is an enormous amount of webbing and one is taxed with the
question what to do first or at all: unwrap it as from the mummy,
sort it and maybe the little ants can still be persuaded to help, fol-
low its loose-leaf strands as they blow thru the arena, neaten it,
perhaps by a traditional weaving, brush it away like gossamer
spinning, hang it all, or some unknown and awkward correlation
of jerky, improvident, undeveloped, and spastic gestures, neuro-
logical overflow in which scryers find a symptom of ("unliterary")
disorders, giving unintended and/or unreadable consequences. So
that—

            "It means

            seize hold of a memory

            as it flashes up

            at a moment of danger."

            hole of a memory

            Get real!

June 1990–June 1991
The Gulf War

Draft 13: Haibun

Drinking Lethe-eau from one spring
Mnemosyne-water from another,

like wine and coffee, opposite greeds
alter the micro balances in the banlieues.
Up and down, up and down
or open and taut, open and taut,
the sand pendulum pattern of Lissajous figures
makes a *here*   always
slightly off-center from the last stroke.

It is unseasonably warm here and the leaves stayed on the trees for
the longest time—even stayed green—for a long langorous au-
tumn, almost a case of arrested development.

Then talk to about silence, in silence.

> A glass of water, a slice
> lemon.
> Golden mountains, silver moon.

At every moment, there are oddities of the journey.

Thursday: found great offense.
Sunday: fountains withdrew.

> Dark and somber dreams of walking,
> low song clouds
> in unbecoming places.

•

"Ever notice tiny specks or strings darting in and out of your eyes?
The Mayo Clinic Health Letter says that although these semi-

transparent bodies, called 'vitreous floaters' are annoying, they don't
affect vision."

> Reassuring.
> Convenience store
> dead air, Flav-R-Pac
> salts it.

The trip, the treck, the record, the haibun-ordinary
details: a high wind, 11:50, blew all the papers off the table
when American haiku extruded from the texture

> walking
> thinking
> bitterroot
> beebalm.

Three blanks, beginning middle and end
Two blanks, thesis and antithesis
Thirst in every direction.
But one learns not to watch
the stately randomness of unaccountable figures.

·

I wear some clothes of the dead, and eat some of the food left in their
cupboards, Vermont maple syrup talismanic,
a soft summer nightgown, use
a hanky with an "E." The clothes survive, and float up
onto this shore rather than some other,
some sour thrift shop rummage sale,
and buying I've had fine linen handkerchiefs, with initials
"WTN" random finds
some dead man's debris
living on after him.

And there are many clothes strewn in the street
Where I walk to work
A pink polyester sweater.

Where?
at close range.

·

The street man pushed his doctored shopping cart ahung with stuffed
and puckered Hefty™ bags. Dangles from the front, one plastic wink,
a bubble "California Raisin."

And the starling, junk bird, slammed into the brick wall during the
storm? Stiff and dead. Cartoon dead, feet out, x's for eyes. And the
grey dog exploded on impact on I-95?

Glisten of bright glass bits. Buffer sofa in the waste spaces, the many
dulls of brown, brush twist total. Denial and remaking. The little
squibs unseen that float thru on the side, travelling out of the frame.
Here, the first 200 patriotic customers will receive FREE American flags.

I should use the pentamenteur line, and organize things better.

·

Experience what the locals already know. Networks of reminiscences
in the reading, constructions of déjà vu, lush chaos

transparencies of the scattering—it is so blown away that it appears
hardly at all, even the residue is invisible, hardly a trace.

So there is no pure art, just something sliding over the site between the
illusion of realism and despair, grappling for a foothold or handhold,
every mark
is made in time, time that is not spent almost weeping and work work
work
like 7 dwarves
all for the moment
of falling away.

Transparencies and opacities slide across each other, pick out each
others' figures and grounds. Words are there, also shaded drawings,

89

muted myopias, floating smudges of mist, brown spores fine and invisible as dust shot off by a little fungus called the earth star. And crossed sticks.

Widen what's wide.
Narrow what's narrow.
Don't bring it to the middle, intensify its reasons.
Some things, when ripped,
need to be ripped more.

•

At 10th and Montgomery, the glass smash where I walk to work, the recurrences of dreck, where I crackle the debris step by step, a sparrow tried to fly up to a linden grappling a doughy crescent of pizza in its beak. Which it had to drop, the choke of crust too heavy

> An octave above
> what chord?

be asking why I am here, why here, why this, why these bonds, why this matter, these little bits of matter *me* and *it,* and

> "the void-strewn firmament"

in which the biggest statue of a Holstein
here to be seen
rises on a bluff over New Salem, North Dakota,
look left,
I-94 travelling west.

•

Being polygeneric, why did all your work behave as elegy?

The landscape bare, without
consideration, without qualities.

"Who are you?"
"I am nomad."

The arking reach of sky, the starry bliss, dew of light, prolix, unimag-
inable but present, in which the traveller wrestles with
flashing visitations of vector

> Quick rumpuses of solidity
> Intercept the endlessly porous.

The Milky Way is "ours" and even we are to the side of it.
And every cell flies up and cries *hark arc*. And "me" a little
blown dust weed seed
whistling, so does it matter if it rise or fall? silvery fibers afloat or
sodden?
No matter how, which way, or why
we drown in the aura of our own joy.

·

One can see why, though, the myth spoke of a Call, "your name here,"
sounded by a Them or The from cruxes of silent bowl-shaped spaces:

Something definite, so to speak.

> Twinkling planets
> night trees net,
> the fireflies drift, the stars float
> as green-bright meetings just above our breath.

There are marks and markers even in the flattest waste places. On my
driveway. Stunned by a few twigs, a dead beech leaf, some crumbling
asphalt shadowy in the streetlight. Whose name did they call? I an-
swered *here am I.*

But who are they? And make a small mark and then, blessedly
(though sometimes the "I" is unrepentent, annoyed),
it
is swallowed into the void.

June–July 1991

Draft 14: Conjunctions

> "Conjunctions have made themselves live
> by their work."
> > Gertrude Stein, "Poetry and Grammar"

1. To write with the formidable consciousness of loss *thus*:

repeatedly emphasized under cross-examination: skin, sky, fog, silence, *and* humility.

To vow to write *so that*
if, in some aftermath, a few shard words,
chancily rendered, the potchked scrap of the human
speck
washed up out of the torn debris, to write
so that
if your shard emerged from the shard pile

people would cry, *and* cry aloud "look! look!"

If yours were the only poem,
the only fragment
left, those who came after,

part of a running script on the running subject
"on the whole unbounded *and* contingent" it
was a truly temporal predicament.
"We seem to behold only a small part

of an infinitely extended structure."

2. "Unconscious in a pool of blood
on the white linoleum floor."

Assailed kosher products, racial intermarriage, the immigrants

just coming in. Bamboo writing, juxtaposition, *and* typographical
irregularity.

Closed circuit at Market East—the flicker
"Supreme Court today"
the dissolve
"create the corporate environment" *and*
tonight's TV, "Number One
with a Bullet."
"Horror & violence do not exceed moderate levels."
You know what I'm doing.

3. Inside the small space I can hardly name
small time jog around the track
6 laps, one *and* one-half miles—
no more sheer opulence—
6 dusky runners, me *and* mine
the miles.

The way *that* can be named is not the way.
But will you take a way that has no name

catch up with
forgiveness?

4. Call this poetics "posthumous."

The articulation of previous silences,
the invention of memory, *and, and but*
the hole, again I said hold,
I have in my head,

yeasty,
a soft brown low scum bubbling
with the tide. *Yet, or nor*
sound be always there,
if you had ears to hear, *or* eyes, *or*
borrow them to burrow here.

A sheet with centers of letters
burnt out? black pages? blanks?
scraps of tongue in combinatoire?
what is "a normal book"?
"Don't laugh; it's paid for."

The social world, they said, "drained from his work"
and didn't say "more's the pity."
Snippets of dialogue?
Syntax torqued?
Stuff roped together on a weekday?
Winking rays *that* scatter?
Speak from the site
as if you were already dead.

5. One bronze tea leaf had stuck to the side
away from the milky sweet.
And, nevertheless, I tip the cup; I rinse it in.

"Can this watch be fixed? It's very good
and very old." Holds it out, gold
to me, the living limen beyond which
she lies.
Shattered, babbling, she
wonders *if* her old watch
can be fixed.
A deathbed.
Still, I can see why it's in her head.

6. Hit the buzzer. Call time.
No one wants mere political correctness, *but*

"I keep trying to imagine the
post-structuralist woman in a supermarket."
I can imagine little else.

The eye-door swings open for me *and* my cart.
Blink rate, you're really on your own now!

7. These pinholes we live
in, the little
songs we sing
stars; twinkling,

so the restless perversities of letters can shimmer
on a lenticular plastic surface.
One thing looks *like* it's fighting or biting the other,
swallowing, tumbling, pecking, *and* electric with pleasure,
the whole poem at each other's throats.

8. *But* we seem to hold only
a small and inchoate part
spread so veiled *yet, or and* fecund,
lavish with daylilies.
Lavender. Orange. Peach. Creamy pink *and* bright.
Maroon, this with Yellow center *and* at the core
a Green eye.
Ribbed, curled, cupped, stippled
and even fragrant, lemony.

One-day wonders
in whose corolla sometimes
alight spicebush swallowtail;
one goddess of beauty
splashing pollen,
the lily her shell.

Or silver streak of neon on a muggy night.
It's *that* poetry
has had brightness, such positive brightness.
It was luminous, *and, or rather or* forgiving,
light pulsing with shadows under the trees.

Time is sizeless.
But, likewise then
someone puts the spoon to our mouths.
We moue *and* juice *and* gum *and* chew.

Something mortal,
stuffed *like* a brico plug into infinity.
Like any half-done job with half-assed tools
it'll never fix it.
Sooner or later the plug falls out
and here

coincides with nowhere.

"To write is to discover this point."

9. Dawn, line, quirk, orthography, abyss.
Pretend it is all margin.

The border, the letters, *as* the page, are white.
It was all luminous *and/or* all destroyed.

Then we will understand *neither*
these arrangements, the small scraps disbursed

nor the act of documenting:
"I'm on record as. . . ."

And not understanding, we will join
them in fear;

fear, *which*, with joy,
is the fact of substance.

10. Go there, go there, go down its numb stair
down the one-way ice-cold track,
steel-folded pilgrim.
Walk shiva.
Stone, pause, margins,
Snow lightly falling freezes your amazement.
Trek dumb
into your number
so you will always remember

in the Gedank-
mal
hall

they gave you,
traveller.

11. I walk, *also, or because* through ordinary objects: tomato
paste, soup spoons; zoo trip permission forms; a monthly trail-
pass in a clip-on holder. Master of the Female Half-Lengths. I
walk to *and* fro, around the island. On which a black *and* white
potholder with a cowface. On which three raw chicken legs, fat *and*
skin to skim *and* pull away. On which a pencil, a lite brite, some
dregs, wedges, crumbs, chockablocks, *and* arrears. Facts in a site of
several important dimensions. No describing the way
it, they does sway.
An octave below what lowest chord, in what terminus for music
lies this rumble?
I wish I were a pair of supremacist red squares.

12. We aim for linkage at 100%, we accept
at a much lower percentage.
Here it is already the debris, animal cuts, paper products,
the float of smaller rectangular
colors called "them" *and* the red one called "that."

The coupage from these mottled views
can they be donnée?

The given? scarce are these words out when
Ferocities of morning unhinge ennuis of night.

To move one foot after another,
to articulate the bread page,
to wave harbingers onto the construction site,
to squeeze the pulp *and* pat it on the deckle
are the works.

13. Not the exotic

that is strange *but*
the small

puzzle coil cup *where* time goes forward
and we try to feel what has happened
and not just to ourselves
and bits of memory float up
vague *and* random compensation.
A kind of scrying after all.

People put down what they saw *or* felt like, there were days designated.
Questions. Lee way. "A fleshy material identity."

It was "anthropology-at-home."

"Some use of one of the harsher sexually-derived words may be heard."

Maps *and* to-scale projections on the desk.
The normal detritus of normal everyday consultants
a-weep over this time
and not just *because* it is time
and they will die in it.

People were spotters.
Sometimes they recorded their acts;
doing, seeing, "crossing, struggling, naming,"
"watching doubting wheeling shining *and* pondering,"
and still, *and/or yet* they were called
"a recording instrument of the facts."

"three weeks old. Permanent brain damage."

"Pair deny charges of case-fixing."

"Let them eat crack."

Were sometimes asked to write
on certain categories of behavior *such as*

"the relation of superiors to subordinates,
and subordinates to superiors."

14. What, then, is the size of the loss?
The size is a triumph.
A chemical glue drying askew
bares the device.
It is called "anguage."
It won't be the same, ever-where
or far away since.

So what is the foggiest notion
you say you don't have?

Anarchist *and* pleasuring
a flowered surface
a surwind on the flood of the sea
splintered bountiful marks.

I throw it all *as* far *as* I can,
and it blows back, blows black,

"a certainty based on the acceptance of doubt"
in "texts at once perfect *and* incomplete."

April 1990 – July 1991

Draft 15: Little

More than that is hard to say.
I am drawing a blank.

High clouds, their errancy, ply over ply,
      float.
      And still
I float on eddies in a rocking enormity.

Not mourning, not pleasure,
but auras of evanescence,
and nickname-painted train stops,
and jerry-built victrolas,
canoes pulling away sloppily from simple docks
dribble and bonk of paddle,
a particular grab of grasses,
hairy stems of weeds,
and the afikomen so well hidden
plus misunderstood
it was never teased forth.
Never then redeemed.

So I saw what I saw,
like photographs of the war,
stripes under wire,
shadows scummed or smudged on pavement,
and starved locked rows.

Some clocks stopped but not
other clocks, tick and tock and
I was part of all that it,
a lucky nothing
not in the way of particular harm,
half witness half witless
      dot—a little
      yod or yid

amid the clamors of dawn,
waking inside the whiteness,
before anything is given—
that is, taken.

To this magic table
spread with glistening nap,
a place like a fairy tale: dolorous and lyric,
"un couvert" where the bread is perfect,
dishes, bodies, fruit piled,
cute mugs caffeine-coated,
wine in dregs and lees,
and salty bowls of weeds,

there is someone, step, step:
over the bridge, down the field,
under the fence, through the door,
and speaks.

The order is "Take cover!"
And hands to necks
the cowering shapes
wedge under desks
puppets of puppets.

Wherein at play
the smallest chancy jot of scratched substance
bounces along a pebbly day.

Recently I lost my watch
dropped straight down off my wrist
and fell into a hole so far it wasn't there.
Strange,
that litmus wristlet π
had covered my nakedness
and now I was exposed.
Or dreamed I'd "missed my stop."

From that point, those points, on,
the trace or shard, the thing

come passing darkly cross me
in the tunnel dirt of time
was mine.

Not hero, not polis, not story, but it.
      It multiplied.
      It engulfing.
      It excessive.
"It" like X that marks the spot, that is, the spots,
an ever wily while, a wilderness of hope.
The spot of almost hopeless hope.
Can barely credit it.

Thus my voice is empty, but I speak and sing
only of this.
The undersentences
that rise, tides of sediment, the little
stuff agglutinating in time, debris
      I sing.
      Cano,
cannot not do it so.

In time's deep well,
my shallow heart has flooded.

From the exile woods
on the edge of the edge
a little mite doth blow.
A Mite! I might
have killed such mites and bits
      before
      today
I didn't think

of needing such
a Little Mite,
this dusty road.

May 1992–December 1992

Draft 16: Title

A wax nipple,
    a simulacrum nipple
        lodged in the slab of a ledger,
the nipple stark
    as a title
        the fusion sealed
            ardor.
The whole riveted to the wall.

Each ledger, for there were a number,
    pulled from the abandoned worksite
        presented an unreckoned order, nipple by nipple,
with the tooled faux-leather corners,
    small shutter scenes, a kind of snap-shut
        shot with 4 black corners, and the faces
so small, too small,
    unrealizable, that one could, so far as
        memoir (or saying anything)
goes, say *the same things over and over*
    time and again, various ways.

Yet time is cast off, cast forth.
    Fleeting *beyond one's wildest dreams*
        The arc of a cigarette butt flicked
out of the moving car in front of mine.
    Even the loss is lost.
        "I am borne darkly, fearfully, afar."

My armada of days taken afloat,
    patient, kicking, counting
        the free-style strokes
up and down the pool,
    but the total unaccountable;
        even into extended telling
consumed, never entitled.

The whole notion of eating:
        eating, eating everything, to get
to the one thing
      that is revealed, an
        avatar of
the poem, which began by being
      organized loosely, but
         here concerns blood creatures.
Avaler,
    a foreign word to say
      gorge on the body of the dead.

So anyway
    "blurred and breathless,"
        the mottled surface of a mortal body
           wasted away.

The sparking arc of a smoked-to-the-filter butt.
      The careful kick, stroke, breathe of the crawl.
      Silences of water.
Cranky bile, books
    like solemn boobies
      bolted to the wall.

A little variety, please,
muthoplokon!
so one may be thrown,
wrestled to the ground limb over limb and,
by the muthe-plucker,
knotted in holds
hobbling folds
over and beyond the bearable.

Thus the panic over the missing codeine, and how,
from that motel, a final short trip
to the middle of nowhere,
could scare up
a prescription of such densities and extensives
that perk and succor

the failing one-breasted body,
a sugar tit of honey suck
one gives the dying—who
could be called?
who, called, could credit
the accident of forgetting.

Just actions, and inadequate summaries:
opening a sealed grim house,
one person in her shallow entry,
that smoky smell of an old motel,
"cottage," "pottage," dank, dark, mildewed.

Yet all that got uttered was
what yard sale and whence
those unfamiliar relics
out of other families' tents—
the flowered butter dish just
slightly cracked,
ancient cameras leaking light—
emerge into unreckonable clutter
at the opening of our tomb.

And "here" the dead with gabble and gargle
pluck sinews one by one, and twist
the terrible tendons to tune
that thrown and fallen pile of flesh
taut as a lyre.

Something will be coming,
some sorry sound.
Of oldest instruments.
But who could credit
such scream, such stream
unsweetened,
thick with unspoken
and unspeakable chords
in the sweet milk of light.

So avaler sa langue, is the expression.
Eat up, swallow, stifle the tongue.
Kashe und shayle.
Questions, more questions,
phantom and evanescent whisps
that evaporate, as if
ashen syllables of Yiddish.

Remember, remember,
remember nothing, but more
than you want to
because following the thread of any one slide
entangles labyrinths
requiring
the rest of your born days
to eviscerate.

A cigarette butt smoking arc'd out a car window,
driver's side puff on the asphalt a series
of dots and disconnections
fire sparks run over
by the next car, the wheels
that ran over the cigarette
of the previous smoker; and the dark car running behind
over the sparky flare
sees it, rolling down the road a little gust,
and then extinguished. Nothing more to find.
Except maybe the unquenchable filter, the threads,
neo-asbestos or polyester,
that catch and muffle, and, finally, fray
in the dump ditch
at the edge of the roadway.

You know the way the cello is so vibrant, and the
piano too,
densities and sonorities that pitch past us
playing hard ball? a shower of desultory fire?

So imagine taking that wood and

slamming it: bam.
Col legno.
What composers in their demonic sweetness
call "extended techniques."

Well, "bam bam bam"
the fist chops the page.
The sound is hardly as convincing
as slugging the cello, gets only a little
rattle, but the gesture——

poetry, schmoetry, it's
dark spurts—it's
words cooked in their own ink:
in su tinta,
which is the creature's blood.

I fall to the tarmac,
filled to the sick.

Given the wrestled
tentacles tendered for food,
given this sauce,
what meat am I eating?
what dark blood letting?
Why this remembering
and that forgetting?
What rears and spurts and thickens
in the fosse?

———————

Now that I'm here,

I'm here.

I'd recognize this place anywhere.

November 1991–December 1992

Draft 17: Unnamed

It's true that every ending only erases the board
rather than filling it.
The poems are written in strange chalk
strange, a chalk
in some lights dark, plump with serifs
on a scumbled, agitated whiteness,
but mainly a white chalk on a whiter page.

Which can hardly be read
and that, only under angled light.

As wide as my life though when you look again it's
a scroll narrow, but fast,
paper towels in the hands of a toddler,
down and up hillocks and rises,
blazes and falls
so fast one can only
trail after it, "what could be more natural."

Or dark as a mist
hanging over the fill-built airport
smoke brown, the sky looks daubed
and of no depth.

But the chalk (with luck, another turn) turns
        translucent, light on light
                which is, in certain lights, like dark on dark
but more
        blinding.

Words,
        scattered falling
                        arcs of shame,
                                glaze the flicker-ridden labyrinth—

it makes a peculiar medium.
                     And its crossgrained nourishment
                     demands a strange tooth.

Perhaps translucence is a quality of erasure.
The thing anyway looks like a Cy Twombly
strokes trailing each other and dibs, nibs,
flicks of the wrist and a dreamy evisceration of pencil.
A morning glory bolted across the door.
My little valise is filled with souvenirs.
And none of them is "art."
I can see why he said I wasn't interested in art.

"Poetry depersonalizes 'days'
in language." It sounded
as if this were what I wanted

yet the hole, the sufferance
fell open. Heard the shaped scream of a duration.
Three times: the same, the same, the same again,
"nothing but these facts and all these facts."
Why did he think I "wasn't interested in art"?

Low song clouds in unbelonging places
                emphasize the activities of light,
                       which is unspeakable.

While the sound, not just the light,
                plays along certain vectors
                     pools in the force field

large, square, rent, timeless
                void. Know?
                     Can barely know what labyrinth.

The grass clods push up
                between the lines and cracks
                     of pavement. In the depth

of night, a street lamp
            looming behind them
                        they rise and lurk,

turf tufts made near twice
            their "real" size
                        by shadow.

But what I meant is this.
            She stood at the pit
                        where, this 50 years,

155 Jews were shot.
            There, near a field of rye,
                        she'd found dozens of notes and addresses

tossed away
            moments before their deaths.
                        To this day,

she regrets
            that, out of fear,
                        she did not pick them up.

The poetics seems plain.
            Since then
                        there are many people spend their time

picking up the notes.
            But they are not there.
                        They are as gone as possible to be.

So the gathering
            is impossible.
                        But still the shapes are bowed,

and search
            this otherwhere of here.
                        Yet had they actually

been there
        that time
                being remembered,

it is equally possible
        they too would have left
                all of them where they lay.

What illusion, what delusion, what disillusion
        writes these gaps?
                tries these missing bits and scraps?

It is not elegy
        though elegy seems the nearest category of genre
                raising stars, strewing flowers. . . .

It's not that I have not
        done this, in life or whereever I
            needed to

or throwing out the curled tough leather
        of the dead
                the cracked insteps of unwalkable shoes,

but it is not the name or term
        for what is meant
                by this inexorable bending.

And it is not "the Jews"
        (though of course it's the Jews),
                but Jews as an iterated sign of this site.

Words with (to all intents and purposes)
no before and after
hanging in a void of loss
the slow and normal whirlwind
from which it roars
they had not ever meant to be so lost,
so little wordth.

There are plenty of reasons to wonder.
Forlorn spirits with spinning "swords of flame"
as much like angels
as it's possible to be, but without
choices or pleasure,
stand empty.
Wavy wheaty heads
dart and sway;
contradictory rages swivel them.
But (pace Rilke) we can tell
these angels, or their simulacra
"things."
Late busses, glass smash, styrofoam containers.
Low sun plain wing
grey Toyota™
ormolu
soccer freshener
kith, soot,
food,
rainbows of oil.

The intersection
by Dunkin'
Donuts, chicken
buckets, milk
and Gulf™ is
where you have to turn
coming
here.

So speak, stutterer, and stain the light with figments.
Rush, and brush, this evanescent shimmer
that does not even track

that does not
even fill or replicate
the historical air clotted here.

And Here
        where all this is and are,
                this back and forth through time,

Alight.
        It's never
                what you think.

                              May–December 1992

Draft 18: Traduction

Pas tout à fait cela.
             Not quite it?
                It's not exactly tha*t*
that A
our edge of it
billows bef*ore* us.

useless, cannot qui*te* grasp . . .

be litt*le s*pot, be draft of
ch*anges*,
litmus rib*bons*
            strips blowing, situés
            roses et bleus,
            flicker . . .

face aux grands enjeux du siècle.

B
Something: an extract or essen*ce* of something
el se; this work pressed onto itself
enfolded imprint,
sleep-writing on a *blan*keted body . . .

Words stranger even to themselves
than cryptograms, like le
or it, ce/ça or see/saw,
always with an inside out, an outs*ide* in,
a so*un* d, a toss,
et la Syntaxe étrange, d'étrangère

to suggest sha*des*

of the unspeakable

Iota. These fragments "conspicuous

orac*les*"

cast off on the silence . . .

C—a task
assuming an exile
of, and in, the world.
Writing defined as
seeing or being
between, for even in one's ownèd language
can see it as translation,
not of text, but of
interstices, blank or overlooked, rough
muddy spots which dogs pee up
this common tuft or
that a black comb was pressed down into asphalt
when all this was repaved,
odd corner, or

if not translation
writing as foreign
from the very first.

Finally, D.
Under the quiet umbra
of the midnight sky a-wait.

The shadow waxing
wonderful to watch,
at once so slow and fast
across the moon.

Yet watching the eclipse I began champing
impatiently. Type A in R.
Taxed by waiting, even in wonder.
To hope any micro-moment will

speed itself forward to the next only accelerates
that whole which goes this fast
and faster still,
this speck, of life. . . .

During which the dark shape
of what we're living on
passes above us,
Galactal smudge.
It's earth. E.
It's where we are,
the wonder is.

Ainsi (A, B, C, D, Etc.) les questions de
traduction se lancent
leurs plaintes silencieuses.

A is for A.
Each thorn and eth,
wirds
you've never seen be-for-
weirds,

> Grandes ampoules
> de plastique
> à moitié flottant dans les eaux mortes des canaux
> objets d'ard, comme a dit Duchamp,
> are swamped.

> Chestnuts, gravel, chestnuts
> semés parmi les cailloux, impossible
> pleasures, crushed.
> C'est marron.
> C'est génial.

All these words have to go into another language;
toute proportion gardée,
where does it mean they "go"?

Go somewhere, that is all.
Go elsewhere
round the dusky dome of time.
Passing over each other, eclipsing light with dark
and dark shimmering with strangeness
so we look, as never be-
fore, at what was
always there—
the inside out of space.

B. Pullulating surges:
scrissi o so
curious and fine.

Ligne de blanc.

Ligne de noir.

League of blank and nor.

Tinier, thicker, denser
than spider webs' wet silver,
blanks and nor—
the text
expressing

un silence, et en plus, un réseau intraduisible
fait comme tissu,

dans lequel quelques JE's et EUX's
se trouvent piégés—
and these
glossalalic trembling wings
snagged in webs of quiet
proposent un spectacle
son-et-mots, un jeu quelconque
where words (mots) bubble, where something
(mut, matte, moot) the mud ferments, and
gets to be another word, mote.

Mote speaking.
Mote spoken.
Bubbles, syllables, galaxies
of babble.

C that C.
À ce moment je mords la langue
quand je rêvais.
Elle est plus large maintenant
que ma bouche.
There are edges and sides
Endges and -cides
it now has it never
had before, it seems

never to have been so large
as now,

swollen, tender, tendus, swilling

LA LANGUE

hard to articulate, slower, but faster
than ever before j'ai passé ces jours
dans une tempête

des petits mots crépitants dont
les expressions ondeuses se font,
auprès desquelles on trouve
au vers
un bon blanc, des vers
qui heurlent
au fond d'un couloir gothique
où des hirondelles en ogive
se nichent juste au croisement
de chaque arc.

I am a black shape moving forward
marging with a black shape
cast like a die upon the stone.

Lettres, j'entre
dans le passage
d'une langue
à une autre,
et de l'autre
à l'outre,
rempli/vide
ici/là
et bien iota/yod.

From all these langu-bytes?
I'm just translating time.

C'Sont des pages noires
avec sidereal speck
a work in hardly any language.
Not of the word, but of the gap.
An experience we are said to have
and the shadow
of experiences we never shall have.
Multiple approximations
of more unstructured, wicked problems.

En plus, E. Etc. It's almost endless
but totally constrained.
It's time, like a path,
littered with the evidence
of nomadic occupation,
these burnished vagaries of use
that I'm after.

I'm after everything, and after nothing.
A belatedness so strong
I come,
even after what is
not there,

after eradication
Who inhabits one's own time

who can be witness
after the eclipse of witness

cannot not speak. O poetry
—again and again no more poetry.

Nothing
is extensive enough
for this level of abandon-
ment,
éminemment macaronique or
marconique, wire-less towers
on a windy shore
transmitting micro-shifts of sound and state-
ment cross a space we do not understand.

"traduire, c'est le contraire"
"de quoi?"

October 1992–January 1993; September 1994

Draft 19: Working Conditions

I.

This kind of speaking
doubles the unspeakable.

With every word
ossuarial shadows.

Come, the gathering. But chancy.
Which randomness is shocking

and may thus motivate more
toward silence than toward speech.

For who can, not silent,
accept the vocation

to acknowledge, to describe,
or even to allow

the enormities

of which one must,
if speaking,

speak.
And the details.

One site cut and recut
twine gridding the sectors of dirt

To have found a grit-filled room
sift gram upon grain

and seek the deep-slung shard
amazing, that any "traces"

once "effaced"
should thereby be "called back."

To have fitted wordless words
inside or over words: for what?

scattered further than dirt,
scattered with atoms, ashes, stars

I live
so in my time

II.

handwriting traces
                              These terms:
                                        traces
"have   *effaced*
            (he said) in the inverse order
                        been (regularly) called back"
                                        and *called back*
(an addled syntax)
with mixed results.

Every word teeming and bereft,
the whole writing
with underspeech parts, incomplete leavings,
offers riddled pockets of inarticulate keens
in shadowy lotteries.

Is then the work lucid and stuttered?
sullied and sullen? startled and studied?
Always, and beyond reproach.

            What's done, is done

and now

Because so evanescent
because their syntax baffles
these words shadow me.

it must begin again.
                The inside-out of space
                a mass of unthinkable matter
            and its minuscule nobilities,
        a dog, say, jingling her tags—
    there's something she wants, something
simple, something she needs to remind us.

III.

Living within
a place where little noises
in wonder at their own skew
hang in the opening.

Carried cavernous
the politics of our time,
insomnias of rage, join them.

On small page self
rose the giant letter moon.
Time is like a path,
but it works on the principle of flickering.

IV.

She wrote: "nothing
        is ever lost. It will recur,"
            but this I did not

believe. In fact
        I thought it
                ignorance of time.

Resistance
    to this (loss)
        in which we are limed.

So many ways to be lost.
    Can barely count
        the ways.

The condition of work being struggle in time.
    With loss.
        And with these random findings.

I resisted initiations
    into "virile pieties,"
        which were everywhere, nevertheless.

But the rage of the mother
    is an unsolved problem
        in language.

V.

Tremped in such conditions—
it's like renting a canoe
and suddenly a windstorm
suddenly thunderheads   A lot of "suddenly"
come up on a lack, I got
lack on the page, but it was really lake, a lake
bigger than it seemed,
at first opportunistic
paddle, and
plunk in the middle of turbulent
atmospheres, where it's just a matter of chance.
She said "look down," as if time were readable
layers, and you could get a grip
map   it, it

to me, disturbances are terms. Crosscurrents

cab here, cab there, mirrored taxis
swinging wildly thru traffic
of the dead
in transit, dead
galore, carryovers from one side to the other
zigzag, fizzle and flare, a series of linked bombs,
orange disinfectant scrub for incision
never any operation but
Thunderheads, lightning from the distance,
green shadow, maternal aunt
starved herself down
65 pounds

"living skeleton."
                                    Later there will be plenty of
Sounds, the dog in the morning yawning: Owwwww—
we say she has said "out."
                                        the word "nothing."
And what other words were to be said off, set off
and what other transfigurations of letters?

"so i had a feeling tonight that nothing i meant to say was over yet

that it was also too late to start

which led me to think i would start later. . . ."

VI.

rondo
junco
window
any color of any thing could speak of that

plate at the shadowy end of the table, green bites

of things, diverse, flecked thru, ambulant, riven

with "multiphonics, circular singing"

and family life, a courtyard of pebbles, raw walls

from a "typical opening and contrasting idea"

road to road so
enter and immense the muddy byways,
the dark clustering
underside.

Even a documentary only stretches so far.

The "inharmonic sonorities" make
as if a piece of time crossed with place had got
brief speaking consciousness,
but has no pronoun and no shape
—not it, nor she, nor me—
so cannot be referred to.

Cannot via well-ruled poem-wedges,
can only flicker at these phatic edges.

VII.

Though it's true that "it" is

closest to it,
all told,

it
was never what I was ready for any time
it seemed to be happening

belatedly
spurts of moment,

dawn winds
that rush around the earth to

roaring place, and roaring time
while small trim sounds go

peep • peep • peep •

which striates my dust-speck

"not boiling to put pen to paper."

On the page the word "recall"
trick of the eye, I read it as "rachel."
Could not follow the instruction.

And the person also
far to the left, something wrong with the capacity for centering
here
almost off the picture
which otherwise is a rectangular piazza in Sweden
a kind of foreign "emptiness"
reminding not so much of space
but of time
will never return.

VIII.

For disappearance is the subject
        of whatever I do.

If not disappearance,
        then what is here.

"During my long nights with these corpses,
        I understood

that they would accompany me
        till the end of my life."

Even at fair distance
        certain photographs

bulldozed ditches in consciousness
        corpses dump into the seam

corpses jump like trout
        backward and forward in my stream.

Still, much will be forgotten.
        Disappearance,
for instance, of crimes
        done for me.
Cheap whatever
        from a monocrop.
Children's clothing
        factory-stitched by children.
Officialdom
        comparatively cordial.

Utopian space
of anger and connectedness
beyond barrier.
And this is the space can never
talk, but
go to
foraging.

IX.

This is the work
This is the work

disfigured

form as experienced

struggle, over the mark.

And over the effacement

tangle conflicting
words, undersides, notes,
disappearances.

Those skeins, extended and tightened,
wound so many years,
have ended (once more)
in an unpickable knot.

One simply present: here.
The objective to say: Here is a knot.
No mystery here.
Not in that.

June–August 1993

Draft 20: Incipit

Curious, this querying letter from a stranger.
   Just when I had in fact
turned back to begin,
   it made me think again
where I had been.

Wash of the day, bitterness, and what observation to make?
   how the basic primal

      luck

of having emptiness on this scale

operated. Or occurred.

Blessed, one could say,
   with a bad, with almost no
      memory,
gifted with it,
   the flower was always
      false forget-me-not,
tender blue, very like the real,
   those sugar'd golden-pinky eyes
      but not right, a lack —

something
   of how the texture of memory
      puckers,
slippage.
  It's never what you think

something—an extract or essence of something else; this work pressed
down unfinished overwritten refolded

iota. That fragments are "conspicuous"

oracles. That the veil of mist behind which stars
shimmer and show
was, in fact, the Milky Way itself, not clouds at all,
                    nor close;
That the diasporic
                    scattering, scattered even in the "home"

talmudic
                    aura of endlessly welling commentary

 folding and looping over

Is.

                    Like it.

                    It is.

And that was it.
It sentenced me for life.

The beginning was, as these things go,
negation. But
'twas also setting forth of signs to read or tell.
Moonlit refraction by a strange heap
counted on base "N" and on base "Y."
Yes and no. Both and and.

And inside that beginning
the no no no set out, unrolled
its grave and merry way,
winding a lane but in a trackless sense
through scudding days, on awe-scratched bumps,
over the design of hills perpetually
blustered with cross-drafts and wind-chills,
spiraling and knotting over itself:
the vulnerable.

Underground, streams of stone
hiss and percolate.
Super-heated gouttes
pop according to the vectors of physics
to form, as they fling,
the drop-pocked texture of time.

It's a cobalt time spent in the wilderness,
ugly lure, and sullen tasteless fish,
guns galore and ready to roll,
which is simply the time here,
time spent observing
small hopes begin the oddities of journey,
time spent hearing
mournful hoots at venomous crossings,
time spent trying
to step step step quivering silver prongs
of struggled tuning.
Time contaminated. Time full of dimension.
Time wrapped in a family of apples,
mourning polished by wonder.
Time again and time again,
that runs clear out
into the starry randomness of scattered far,
way beyond the articulate limits of syntax.

Pause   space   work   space,   inside emptiness
                    to write is to drown, rip tide, rip time.

Pause work, false work, milky work,
                    time and tide in wait for nomad.

Aged dog, her murky running eye—
                    dawn time, even tide.

Nits and gnats, snits and snats, born for the minimum,
finite, finished, fermished
and dead in a minute,
into the air a little spill

as invisible dust-threads spot shimmering down
and swim in beams of ever-mobile light,
named fixedly, obsessively,
tenderly, "hunger"
to honor who and what we are.

What a joke. What a job

endlessly
to research objects, colors, items, targets, designs
caught in the mottled crossfire of time.
"Those were gunshots huh?"
"Yeah an' your dead"
and so they were,
unmistakable,
with a nervy echo.

———

It's because I ran out
of paper that I'm writing this
on another draft.

So here and there
a stranger word
comes through.

It being the only canvas
wide enough for human sadness.

October 1993–January 1994

Draft 21: Cardinals

N. Letters on familiar matters

Small site:
    inch square cancelled stamp and why
save those pretty timbres from elsewhere, that
    they have been on a journey? and ended? landed?
Letter before the storm
    leaf sides twisting, folded in a thick green light.
Mummified in the eaves, perfect bird
    skeleton, the roofer wanted it and took it.

Taken as literal.
    The small words, written in pain and rage
that marked her latter
    existence. That were its
guarantors. Four lines
    into the inchwide day space
allotted in those calendars,
    Renoir et Cie,
plump with situational irony.

    The unsolved problem, rage
of matter. Pencilled by the livid mother.

^ ^

The fact that the room, fresh painted, was entirely empty,
whilst the house
was not, made the room the site of the dream.

Someone flat as paper lies in that room
whose shelves are blank.
A sego lily — white, writ purple in the calyx.
Taboo, tight stairwell.

In the thin space
the maternal tower.

In the window, 2 globes.
The distortion of glazing twins vision
like the strabismic moon you'd see
double-edged, teary-eyed on a windy walk.
Globe upon globe,
the reflection doubles intent.

"But with Schönberg, affability ceases."

An implacable canopic jar
contains the shambles

a broken watch, "can't it be fixed?"

a leaky camera taped, "perhaps valuable"

depression glass:

Plans to elaborate, lost.

^ ^

These are, then, ghost pieces.
Dust caught in an indent in the woodwork.
Tie shots of fetish objects. Overlap
of time, a fold in place
as if a camp joke in the prissy pines,
vast once, the dirt path steep, will "always remember"
had said
how muddied with clay the roadrock was.
But now?
What to ask, and of what past, or path.
Some texts conjure memory.
But for N., the continuous negation
of memory in Lethe
is the, albeit intermittent, task.

E. Diary of days that may have existed

Waking at dawn to hear the penetrating
rain, rain seeping into time
lavender-grey patches of the changeable

I have become the mourner
somewhat of a change.

^ ^

Would you exchange
for this sodden, rusty territory, for
snow tinted with a pink melt chemical
and crusted soot?
For these warming sediments of unfinished business
which settle and then
float again, colloidal, which slide
and toss, which seep and leak
saturated with debris?

Exchange what?

^ ^

It's time like a path
littered with items from nomadic
occupation, the burnished vagaries of use.

Yet at every moment one encounters
direction-saturated cardinals
in rose-splayed constellations.

So much, so many, yet, in a cold E. light,
resentful, embattled, and empty.

Stream of nonsciousness, an
emptiness on this scale astonishes,

given that salty pacs
of food engineering
do fill you up.

Articulately sprayed: so

WHAT THA FUCK

YOU LOOKIN AT?

∧ ∧

"absence of what qualifies this surface?"

There are sublime fields of color.

There are uncountable ranges of failed excess.

It is hard to situate, hard to encompass direction,

call it "true north" or

"true blue," whatever.

What's to find in the woods

anyway? The news says

the body of a woman has been found.

The point of this statement is crude,

like a statement about concrete barrels of dreck

packed "with acquisitions, consolidations,

spinoffs, mergers, and layoffs"

being dumped, with calculation,

deep in the everlasting ocean.

S. The translation of betweenness into betweenness

"'On foot,'" said S.,
"'I had wandered up and wide
thru galaxies and stars
before I'd even plucked
at the loose red thread
of my red, red dress,'

but once I'd picked and pulled
a little play of the side seam,
worrying it, with its unstuck overcast bit,
trying to unravel stitches into thread,
once I had taken that wrinkling thread
and picked and pulled,
and pulled and picked,

I found that constellations
and blood-red sprigs of tensile lint
suffused each other and intertwined.
Once I had tinkered and twisted the red thread round,
once I had attended solar systems with their unfathomable time,
it was cardinal pleasure;
I sought more of the same,
somber surface of one red dwarf,
its lush, atom-laden namelessness,
and red selvedge into the labyrinth."

W. Atlas of the rufous earth

  The biggest disorder of time
is memory's frayed existence;
   "a disorder of memory" is memory itself.
The continuous encyclopedia
   with its categories unformed

its indices unmade
     its alphabets unorganized.

In the backyard, a consistory gathers
     to elect the next moment,
tufted, coral-beaked, doubled doubles.
     Males, bright raccoon on red,
females, some days iridescent
     a pinky greenish brown,
others, a buff, dull, moody fluff.

The point for W. comes down to
being a hinge, constructing oscillations
adequate
to shock and to recurrence,
taking
words from before, words from after;
replaying
for new pleasures of preposition
words
that never were from anywhere, yet
form place
irresistably, and further, at the site of repetition,
form changes.

^ ^

It's 4:32 exactly.
A terrible dream, but one
not impossible now for girls of ten:
"bad people coming into the house"
and will not wake to tell what happens then.

Here and there, day and night I walk out into
the least particle of astonishment
in which nourishment collects.

But whatever there is to say,
     a vibrato among the cardinals

splits words at the point of their affirmation
  casting the bits adrift in syntax
    half in and half outside the compass of silence.

May 3, 1993–May 23, 1994

Draft 22: Philadelphia Wireman

Red "8" dreamscrip double
travelling red "8" inside the train; these twists *are twinned, are*
tricky tracks following the trail of any conjuncture, fused in the yard
where signals web, and spoked electricity
spooks furrows, making kaolin

the moon.   HOW, what is this HOW
by silverleaden street lamps,   ordinary site,
that debris insomnia   topographic extreme, cool lit   MADE.
Spurts and flecks of dirt along the baseboard. Red number shadow
registers neon fizz.
Twisted together
scratch, gum, mite, dust, web
agendas; the overspill
exilic.
Possessed forsaken bridges
asymmetrically, wherever   *debris insomnia* trebled

ordinary stuff
extreme, cool lit
Junted *agendas* that twine their *hinge*

scratch, gum, mite, dust: travelling the range of signs.
Grunge things junk things, things singed by light.
HOW hung the hinge from void to word
from word to work   the rage *of signs*
from work to bode   *asymmetrically*
wherever *agendas* TRAVELLED.
The detritus
lucking the traumscrapt: lucking
transcript, trauma, script, and scrap. How scraped down to
radiobones—*spurts and flecks* of awe, and joy-
rigged jerrybuilt trash dense ovoids   zig-filled zeros
forsaken bridges:
So much for structure, triple,

odelike, but *twisted together, fused*
the same, the same, the same again.

Had wound already *radio*-text — hinging welds
for reels and rolls of silver. Ratiocinated lap joint. Lapis.
Foldit the wire. Foaled OF.
Did OF again.
Heard the mixing of the tracks   *red "8" inside the train*
did mop microchip matting more and more
from woof to bode.   Did lapsed card, bent
pin, phillips screw, pop top, junk spot, knurled nut,
and plastic stirrer down by the loading dock.

HOW, what made from Cars, acceleration, crushed cans *Who*
heard the mixing of the tracks and chose to shunt the folded twist

that
wires systems, that cycles cyclonic light. WHO MADE
chromatic models impossible *webbed* down in the rest
who circulated zigzag workings   *filled zeros.*
WHO DID the work?

Clusters of electricity and notation
from the dump ditch
but mum's the word.

Glisten of bright glass bits
thru the work dirt, making, of
green and white wire, of silver wire
voracity part of terror
of thick brown electric cording:

In signage and binding
work the working
in budgets of mismatched numbers
colored rubber bands wrapped, and *OF AGAIN*
wrapped this, wrapped this, wrapped this
mummy
of wattage,
wire wadding inside TV backs crushed and matched.

Raygun downtime wire
wound round talisman. *Can you tie*
Hard store spiky columnmojo
talismum   circulations
of wrapping.
Bottle-cap, bracelet, bundled scrap, conductor wire
tape ribbon condensed ballast erased ballads *travelling the rage*
of signs.

Wrapped this, wrapped this, wrapped this, wrapped this
in the upbuilded.
Allegro, largo, presto, dominato, and elegy.
Cifar, naam, vak, datum, klas,
plastic, glass, package, trademark, umbrella,
batteries, pen, leather, reflector shatter,
cellophane, spring spirals, filigree naturewire,
cap nut, square nut, wing nut, lug,
bolts and clamps, telephone listings, bulb sprok,
nails, foil, coins, toys, watch,
tools, trinkets, tickets
AND quivering filament.

Can you tie up Spirit Writing *the hinge from void to word to work*
on the wadded page randomize the flow of paths.
DO *bottle-cap talism-*
um ur flicker inside the upbuilded. Be *in the* OF
and MAKE deep spurts from depths of cursive scrimmage.

Electrodynamic powered surge. *Can you tie*
up round bent, wicked wrinkled
wrung out, folded up
time to do it
in.
Stroked electricity. *Chromatic*
conjunctures hingeknob crushed
HERE. and HOW.
Cans glittery sharp. Spilling onto the street.
Flicker inside the upbuilded
bits. *Foldit* matter

dreckbundle wireloaf static mingled whirlwind
                    wound whorl work.
                                   Street light greeny-silver
                                   glittery sharp. Play "8."

          40 greyish watts across the way. *Can you*
                         pin to place ELECTRIC
              websaw system, *tie*
              IT from the square-law curve of light,
mark another point OF, dots, *can you tie*
              flicker and hiss, neon spark rune *can you tie up*
                         the anger
                         of the dead?

                                   March 1994–August 1994

144

Draft 23: Findings

1.   Pretty difficult to say, finally,
if it's loss or gain that is the subject; they are so
mingled, as
      someone sleeping is mingled up, in it
without knowing it.
      A tangle of night sweats

      maybe falling,
      on edge.
      This could be the finding.

            Penis wiles, link and unlink.

            Small hot moon
            now set.

2.   Possible to say
"it was shot hand-held."
Just so—jerky, as they ran or fell,
something about the film speed
which exaggerated rhythms: took it slow
and played it fast.

Splots of meta-light on the old film—
an empty celluloid flash streaks the picture
randomly,
and light is even more ambiguous
in the dream.
Because one cannot say from what source or space
that beamy dream light streams

      quietly over a misted lake
      feathering oars.
      Angelic.
      And J? does that interlocutor

stumble over the hard-bit shingle?
squeamishly slog thru
lake-compost up to the ankles
just to get "in" to begin with?

3.   Delivered
came a ghost letter, typed, but not with ribbon,
so only the pressure of letters
was left, white incised, take a look, it's in
long paragraphs, but the sheet solid blankness;
and beyond "hard to read," erasing its palpability,
and beyond the fact
it is impossible to read at such length
inside a dream is
seeing a glimpse of what forever
could be of
words, but was in fact words never.
Yet even losing it as I skimmed
and the insult of loss shadowing
my ebbing tries, still I looked forward then
now to decipher this token of care, wanted
badly
to read it, meaning to me
so much that it had come thru the mail,
a corresponding letter, but without black letters on it,
so black to blank it went unrolling back,
with the
"in" from invisible,
the deeper double "in" and "in" from finding
and made a dissolve.

Thus the message was lost, yet
an atmosphere enveloped this space from now to not
from not to knot and non- and back and forth
to now
in which the letter opened and declared
(direction indeterminate)
what it was, and what it was to be.

Signed,
in his inimitable handwriting,

4.   I am not in it at all.
All the shadowy interlocutors await the setting down
of any mark.
They will jump
stark in the crevices of dailiness.
The prying, the twisting, riddle and edges suddenly being
moved to rigor, tears, astonishment, rage, luminosity. These
can barely be organized "in"
anything. Washes of color across time? Ebb,
flow, and lee? Pictures of so-called
"things" (a rock, a boat, a gnarled bush) floating
across enormous scrolls
whose creamy whiteness is made to stand for
mist and mist and still more mist, in which
nothing, essentially, is visible?

Given: a week, the original cluster of seven wanderers, one day
after another, this and that "lyrical diary";
Given: a multiple of weeks, a pocky
twenty-eight blaze lunar path;
Given: an alphabet in twenty-six;
or Postulate the twenty-four
planetary hours, each invested by a chronocrator,
"the Angel or the Power that rules this hour," with no telling
what schemes,
or Propose a finite number of random things, which have nonethless,
as sorts sorting,
fallen just so for now:

and by coincidence, for it is 4:32 exactly,
darkly.
Delicate, the digital descent of three simple numbers.

5.   So. These pinholes.

Hear the wind.

        This instruction — without question —

as clear as it needs be.

6.   Rusty fungi, lichen-sided trees, grainy granite,
dots in time
which one could gloss over and over

from the vulnerable dissolve
from the waking discharge of darkness
from there to here — an old measure of holding.

It's as if the whole is an ark
everything doubled, adrift, and
overshooting landmark.

Moved speechless. Between each word
there is such space, whole years to the day
prolix nekuia,

To the day itself, to the very day in which awakening
blue estate, fourth wall, there are attested facts,
tinny whisperings stating time, news, accidents.

7.   A bird plate,
a bone-handled knife,
a cow mug,
tender things,
inventorying just
those special to here.

All unevenness and yelling up
and down stairs — what
message — sneakers — come on!
A dashing road —

being on it, nothing
too small—red line, three dollars, egg bagel,
sock hole, pattern whine, chipped glass.
That loop in time between "hurrying"
and "postponed"
which is now.

8.   For filaments
already spun, hang, hung and
were already blown and flung
billowing junctures
from roof to plant, from chair to car
to porch, tree, pail, table, and bush,
multiples that cannot
attach the points there are
however many hypotenuses
one postulates, that go cross every X
and every T, that triangulate
even things one cannot even note.

9.   Dance, accepting a good deal of dancer sound.
Squeaks, wet pants, huffing the beat, and spin.
Take talismans, pilgrim, and lay them
invitingly across the blank
white-black mine in which light holding my hands so

touchingly in one arc throw the die into time
the spotty body falling by chance, and again, bet.

That's how I walk.
That's how I talk.
Oh baby, that's what I like.

10.   Entering under the lintel of the alphabet
in the epistolary mode
I write with letters in letters, and
the correspondence intensifies
from one to one.
Some texts conjure memory one full day.

But the restraint of the rememberer
is so bold that fissures and fragments
compete with finish.
What "little" epic monuments?
What "flash" lyric memory?
What mazy feminine boxhedge, trained so?
What mythic press is this?
What struggle to escape?
Why am I so hard on poetry?

The trail is broken, and the sound skein
loosened and tightened
threads an unpredictable way.
Orion way off around, and under
below the west, has turned, as a matter of course,
since November, and his enormous X,
the fuzzy clutch of sisters at his belt,
and the strong corner stars shining eons of vibrato
are folded away for now.

A milk seed blowing, thus contrite the remembrancer
considers the milky baby-hairs of time.

11.   Wet rails, and the oil of crushed leaves.

Forget sententiae.

Just a button by the curb.

That extremity dilates vision, I can barely
walk where it is, registering
the vectors, its self, its sewer,

its user, its loser,
their possible pattern, to repeat
it (or in) again,

cast into chance, give them odds,
it's all or nothing

with modifications.

Typing loose; getting losse on the page,
to repeat it again.
Is grande randonnée—a walk down a trail—

linked to random? or is it all
sets of linked modules, each logical
only to themselves.

But with the "d" on my keyboard
sticking and "ifficult" to register
because of the sticky weather

I got on the page "linked moules"
which authorizes a double homage
to MM. Marcels Duchamp and Broodthaers.

Absolutely not the same idea as the
zoom in on the button.
In fact, it's totally opposite,

but both are present
never- and
nonetheless.

12.   Non. Say it "known," that is "none" as nones and tides
a certain prayerful force.
Say it "non-"—as noncombatant, nonparticipant,
and fear again, as during the so-called Gulf War
of wearing even a scrap of noncompliance or resistance
because of the ferocious "support"
itself perhaps just support for a "fast action"
and bringing the combatants
home to engulfment in our usual lives.
Now suffering from the deformities of
their recent children,
chronic malaise, nervous system totally shot,
falling apart at the touch,

from inexplicable untracable nonfocused or inadmissable
agents inciting
chemical or biological
Aceldama-rich damage.

Understand complicity and cowardice.
When little yellow rosettes and flags
are sported in a certain
atmosphere, can barely speak

known, and non- or "non!"
the French for NO
"we should have known"
or said NON!
faster?
Being powerfully sorry
being unspeakably sorry
now, let me count the ways.

13.   Cricket cages, summer and autumn,
airy or warm, encouraging song.
Tiny cricket-plates for dinner,
porcelain, depicting aphids.
Cricket beds as snug as boxes
cricket poems inscribed inside them,
just the ticket for insect reading.
Cricket rings for bouts of boxing,
and long brush-like cricket teazles
to push them to the ring and make them fight.

14.   These quirky manifestations.
Incidents of a time, spare and concise.
Vines rusted to the trestle.
Six hours of sight-lines and
the "and" of Williams.

A capuccino smell.
And more.

You're looking at this space right now.
So put "your basic message" right here.

15. It's a cup, a plate, junk mail,
a dribble from the dog's mouth,
Gettysburg, from the library,
in the Landmark Series,
shin guards, scrap of paper
with raisin bread, blue cheese, and 438–9953 in 215
with multiple arrows vectoring off.
A clothespin moved from here
to there; after five days
it's put away,
the clarity of little occasions
for sorting.

16. That findings be
a kind of renga chain, circulating with oneself.
An in-depth counting.
Still to have said
"moon," "constellation," or "the change to autumn"
enough and in the elegant cycles of association
effortlessly,
is not possible right now.

17.   Basement corners, storage, cellar powders
        the accumulation of stuff impasto,
                doors, boards, tubs, wires, ropes, paint, shelving, foldups
interior wasteplaces
        articulation of sliced trim and trash wood, dehumidifier, yes,
                here's stuff plenty handy.
Dark Hill. Iron Stack. First Day Lake.
        and Red Floor, White Floor. These wee keeps.
                tenderly of the used,
"at once natural and industrial,
        crude and refined,
                gritty and elegant"
Not quite my findings.
        But, given everything,
                they might as well have been.

18.   Couscous. Arugula. Bulgar. Mango.
Pesto with pine nuts. Tomatoes, basil, oil.
Rosemary. Foccacio. Ratatouille. Capuccino.
Garlic.

Romaine. Danish blue.
Coffee ice cream.
French bread. Apricot jam. Raspberry seltzer.
Carrots. Turmeric, fenugreek, cloves.
Seltzer with lime.
Garlic.

Bagels. Saga blue. Goat.
Olive oil. Frying peppers and feta.
Salmon. Chicory and Boston. Arugula.
Cannoli, sage, and garlic.
Pasta. Pesto with walnuts.
And garlic.

Locatelli. Canteloupe. Salsa on jimaca.
Corn chips.
Jersey tomatoes,
basil and olive oil. Sour dough. Penne.
White from Orvieto.

Arugula, zucchini, broccoli rape,
granny smiths, spinach fettucini,
green beans with soy sauce,
vanilla yogurt, croissants, strawberry jam,
and garlic.

Bananas. Greengage.
Black. Italian prune. Wheat pilaf.
Trout au bleu.
Watercress.

Capuccino. Capuccino. Capuccino.
Fresh lemonade.
And garlic.

19.   The qwerty keyboard was invented
to slow the typist down
so the individual letters
would not clump and jam.

It bears no resemblance, as you intuited,
to the frequency of letters used in English.

And your funny writing—
well, Mommy, you have
unreadable writing too:
look at that "ing"; it looks like a "y."

20.   Through the light, a glisten and shining
the streaks' diffusion intense inside the lens,
looking up from textual reproduction
o language, language,
fingers caught in black and white beside the poem.

There is enough to look into
here for the rest of a lifetime
the while whisp whittles of syntax
how to make the language draw

up, across the "contours"
(the way of beginning
as if all over again), these
diaries of hours that may as well have existed.

21.   About rhumbs, gradations on the compass rose.

A silent turning in all directions

drawing attention to its shape: circle, vector and box

silence, emptiness, dumb

diminishing, suddenness, fear,

void, gradations, swings,

wind shifts, wind chill, wind shear,

factors, statistical probability, cab brnt, mn ded

flt scttr

look out where.

Boxing, turn that magic wheel, round and round

and random, some spurt, some pulse, some phrase, but what and where:

Could be a particular kind of "R" like a "rho,"

rhapsody, rheum, rhythm, rhododendron, rhyme.

Why here, why this, why now, why me, or no?

That's what I have to say.

The word itself, with its rh- and -umb,

jostles the memory.

22.   Engulfed, each night,
with tsunami from the vibrant void
of sky and space,
from the implacable emptiness, or unfillable fatedness
of all spires, cycles, works, words, worlds, and wires:

Thus. To be so. In is.

23.   The experience of thinking
of one's own absence. Of one's
randomness.
Whatever brought you in
to being, and the little

chances, the accidents
of the living
"missed, but not by much"
"any nearer the artery"
"no helmet, but really lucked out"
"105.9, she was burning up."

Black speckled night,
the generous enchantment of being
in shadowy places,
and hearing whispy contingent
whirlwinds suddenly twist the leaves
of that branch over and over,
inside the unremarked extent of unknowable time—
but none other on that tree.
And on no other tree?

24.

"strange hours"

                    "we keep"

That is, our lives.

                                    July–September 1994

Draft 24: Gap

Not under the clarity of the perfectly black square
        articulating pure erasure
where time or speech be emptied under the power
        of a power, the pwer precisely to quadrant the square
and indelibly to color it, acquiring points and promotions
        to higher pwr for the (dark) neatness and the (darker) lucidity
and the (darkest) completeness
        of the orderly achievement of erasure
(in our time),

but a thread
        twisted tensile yet sprung unweavable
a seam
        breaking inside existence
a vent
        that flanged

through dark, and between
  a wander, all awander
        fracture and hinge.

One asks for meaning
        and, faced with any bit of fleck along the crack,
is eager: is it
        in that spot, can one care
for it, is it there?

Now is the now. No matter what. No readiness
for its ungrouted forms.
Meaning is in its lack and in its bet,
in trips that trigger rime.

Let these be called the (underwired) "chips
      of messianic time."

Then: Let coat collections for the cold. And what
        sleeveless passages are, what tunnels
                iced by neon
trudged,
        steps echoing among statistics, and what
wanderers are,
                between hold and hole
                        among the mille-letters' shifted marks.

        Who sits at the table when policy is set?

        The girder amid, within, among, above
over, on   as if   I had been shot in the head   that day
between   the rickety boards,   the middle of city nowhere, in
                construction, before visiting   the locked ward
sight-reading the interface   when the   potential antagonist
at the innermost court did not strike.   Or so they said.
        Did not yet strike with full intent. Dd nt,   or strk
                a never (mean, a nerve), the   deep never
                                of the river   of parallels.

                                Inside the wish the thick walled house
is useless.   No one can date blankness   Can one
from distant fragments turning   date it, the numb
        greyland gunmetal drypoint?   count fissure as vision?
                        number nullus?

Shadows of the lost, can one want to touch the lock,
siphon the lack,
and push that door a little crack? or not?

Frenzied with mere pinholes of opening, letters
        flooded into the space like paint
                and soaked the site
                        with unreadable stain. But nothing
heroic, nothing but
tacky shadow piles of
nous and nouns,
not irresistible, but chronic,

set among a greyish fog so deep one cannot compass where one is,
in the lost and found
of aphasia, which makes such wwords you never heard
and pain to hear,
such periphras "that thing you know, like uhh uhh uhh, what
you do that with"
or "with that"

that plunge us further into the irreconcilable.

Was there a choice?

>   The specific densities
>   of what happens or follows. As it
>   does, it does.
>   Unfolding gentle garlands of sound,

>   little phases that went nowhee

>   not a random place,

>   but a shadow face.

Unsayable, unsolvable—the whole is built on them.

The dispersion of letters across everything one touches
as if thousands of pages
were only prolegomena
to itself.

The question
>   just of "r."
>   Dead, or dread,
it marks the distance
>   that the particulars scatter,

which if attended
>   would mire the watcher
>   in unparalleled mourning.

For "historical dead"
is what   she wrote, but I   split down the selfsame question
had written "historical dread."

Therefore there is no volta,
writing being mired forever, or whenever, in its own
inky letters,
        missing and present,
                winding and unwinding,
segmenting indefinitely,
                error, placement, gap, and spell.

Some now more voiceless side is even there,
        as maybe dropp a letter from your name
                but which one should you,

                                ache l?

October 1994–February 1995

Draft 25: Segno

Memory makes twins
  from single rocks.
     Similars that materialize
maybe a little
  behind the other,
    one walks the path
bound into forgetting
  and suddenly stumbles on a rock.

Twin from a single
  amnesia,
     grainy speckle of granite,
each and every tittle
  a mirror to double
the forgetting
  "what cannot be spoken."

What cannot not be spoken
  deep in one letter or the other
    bits of line or angle
making now into not:
  this being the t/w of poetry,
    the veery space for shifted marks.

Mourning, risen on the cusp
  of the squandered, doubles
the unhouseled wanterers
  with their unleavened shadows.

To articulate each teacup,
  acorn play plate or play food, each
    child in dress-up, a gypsy, a witch

they were; they were

foreign and distant what I mean is
          near and constant

drained, a vapor

flares.

No matter who was walker,
          who was not,
                    all moved along the toxic
path shrouded in silence
          twigs bound up in ragged canvas,
                    fuel incipient.

Could hardly
          put foot down and lift it to the next simple
                    for one foot dragged the other's dread.

Dread of the children falling,
          dream saults over the precipice.
                    Dead! says the voice, and one
wakes up
          miming her death as "dead"
                    within the dark space of action.

Thereupon said: "they spun, swung
          me over the side of the precipice to fall.
                    I fell, concrete wall
fell fall,
          down withal
                    to the litter of children sent before.

And that was I, forevermore."

The dream-eye behind the real eye
          tenses up,
                    anticipating impact.
The dream-speech of the dead
          reverberates, a tunnel of echos

in a regress of implication.
There was absence stalking déjà vu called
jamais vu, in which what
now should be
familiar, is not.

Of living in a landscape whose flaring cries
are not sound, are
cries not to be cried
but atmosphere, ache and el,
their world-renowned interface

to be remembered as such.
A task deep within restlessness.
And thus the story, o

the story—

a twist of the die in the hand,
a hiss of luck, and they're off!

The claim that for "I" or "you"
would come the substitute
"lamb" or "ewe."

Yet in effect it was
"you" snarled in the barbèd site
who burned in place of "I."

Luminous globule of redgold poised on the tip of the pipe

blown   blown   blown   a blaze of thinnest glass   in fire broke.

Who then can (now) (or not)
think like a lyricist
the wood thrush warble,
those hidden nesting tones
the leaves that piping whistle
hist to every whisp,

though it all does exist—
        the round earth hanging
                a dewy blue-green leaf
in the space whose amoral pressure
        and whose whole elements
                engage me like a gear.
I am spun whirring
        and can say no more.

                                        – – –

Erratum.

There is, however,
a continous addendum
in the name of Erato, muse or must,
livid and singed with signs;

mine posing moments of gloss
on the text of loss
that has long been set
and has been set long:

one conjuncture of ash,
one girder of smoke,
hovering, still,
over rubble also of smoke.

                              May 31, 1995–July 31, 1995

Draft 26: M—m—ry

That the airy opening hung somber,/ that the moon
trapezoid/ on the floor be thus, be/ here,
        that musical/ logic in
   the hypnogogic space/ come waves rush/
                 crosswise, athwart they
suspend opaque/ particles, sand
               versus translucence,/ and that this
filled/ void, this exfoliated down fold, volatile,/ asks for "rachel
             back,"/ in subjunctive
       sentences/ within the earth's inward
  narrow crooked lanes/ and startles who, or what, that
      with me/ tripped the limen and was caught/ Here,
           maze of a maze, the/
         she and I, the I/ of she "back from where"/ were
dazed amid the real/ world, the real real world/ inside which
this "guaranteed destruction/ of papers and files" exists;
        happens as such/ the service
          advertised that this company provides.

We have reviewed / the document — a one-Page Memor-/
andum — Plastic ribbons blown/ blowing on
      the twisted/ twigs
        of 1995 be any
tree/ by any roadway, every day,/ the
          wish will flood/ such shredded flags of loss/
             and have determined
the variable/ space, feather, point, gleam, spume,/ midge
      streaks readable or not.
    More than that?/ *that it cannot be declassified/*
           dim dawn-long day, twi-grey/ mostly
I just marvel/ at mild blue
     watercolor/ light
        a struggle/ between voices that compete/ to
identify what I want/ and other voices/ whose
       high twists cannot be/ remembered

       or released in segregable portions./ It must be withheld
that spoke/ of a hand erasing/ across the mind collective/
                   hope in the photograph/
                   she did not look like herself/ she said/ tho she did
she'd half forgotten/ what we did, we did
                all that/ two decades whited out/ static
"that short/ of a time." *in its entirety/*
on the basis of the (b) (1) and (b) (3) exemptions of the FOIA.

It's just time/ a soft unreadable light
                sweet/ wax in wane./
      Poetry the opposite:/ it's always given out/ the fact
               that it remembers forever,/ good at deigning
memorial design:/ this pile-up of letters—
                   don't do me/ any favors,
           since, as the site/ of detritus and forgetting,/
one could not want to see it bettered.

     An explanation of these exemptions/ is enclosed.

                   Raise and lower the frames/ to lock
          jacquard./ Aubergine robes, filmed
herself thus clad,/ ghosts of the homeless/ at the windshield.
Lives/ in furrows unspellable/ mnemosyne misty over
         the field (misspelled/ as filed), its empty/ dashes
declare a signing gap, singing/ gap of herself hello again
               unpronounceable/ mnemosyne:
       blanking out in extreme/ sadness, bartering/ liquidity
          to hyphenate the cracks/ because
     they mark/ a bridge to
             particulars one wants "forever."/ Marjoram
             the tiny. Hyssop the twirly. Basil/ the tangy
                 in time stuttering
             mn-mn-mn-/ cold morse/ dash dash
    and sputtered out, the guttering flares/
              gone ash.

This is a velocity of signs.

Small yards and all that infrastructure lying bare, beating still.

Train bridge, boulevard razor wire, resignation wholesale.

The many moons of Jupiter and other parts in a kit, the universe

soft in our hearts, who go the road of the unsayable

under phosphorescence, the stars and planets made little

enough for us. Here.

On her cake the "e" in "years" got smudged. Two full

dreams to catch the train

just left. Could barely decipher

the veering of half-spoken, stubs

of the uncanny outcropped along the track,

dead and living yoked together that harrow

shattered shadows and dim light, their immeasurable

desires indignant for name.

Take it all as a loss.

Begin anywhere.

August–October 1995

Draft 27: Athwart

1.

There was an other side
    a space behind, in back,
an overmuch, an
        into which
where muffled voices throb without their names.
        It, whatever the term,
    falls out of range
        such regular registers
as corporations,
    justifications,
        orchestrated bailouts—
        basically, what computes.

Screening odd stuff curled in the can
    all of it strictly rushes,
    it showed drive, but drifted into derive,
    hardly a "ray focusing"
        anything to a point,
    hardly
        what needed to be considered.
    Cheerfully "now," a callow vector,
with the before missing, the after inconsequent.
    Twenty years here,
        twenty there
            flare
            and go frail.

2.

Unsolicited mourning
        floods this site
    a well of muted consciousness.
    Connaissance inutile.

Do you make it *useless knowledge?*
helpless
understanding?
or *unthinkable recognition?*
Untranslatable it
is the transverse torque
across this course.
A lost specificity:
not documentary, not song,
but a wall;
"the" evoked, but what's to point at—
incomprehensible zero space?
the ledger's incalculable underside?

An execution usually "over there,"
some last words that
frame the poisonous cavils
of the general listener
who modifies and justifies
who disclaims and denies,
but basically can't stop
going along.

3.

Next day, cyclonic rains,
from which the tree,
an oak of sixty feet
and sixty years, fell down.
A tilted force pushed through the winds of ferocity.
Its final muffled noise and muted rush
were quick,
a surprise how reverberant,
how hard to assimilate.

Ragge of verse
buffeted by high roaring
                                        deep
negation, hole/hold can sometimes split and pivot,
can create subjunctive hope and affirming rhetorics

that it may be protected! so provide
a giant hand to dust tree off and root it deep again!
from flake to shape remake irrevocable time!
Give us a shallow dent of dirt in which to prop!

There was a time
up thru November 10
wherein the tree
just was, its oakish life
as such.
One storm and
one thud. It's the work of a moment.
An "event."
Something live from the winds
that empties "is"
of its simplicities
and pours "it" as libation on the ground.

4.

Within the concert of the known
an errant sort
gets thrown, whereupon
largo twists itself
into capriciousness.
The event lists,
for the soloist,
inside a labyrinth of forgetting,
can not fake it any longer.
His hands fall athwart.
His memory has emptied.

The lapse looms large adrift
belongside what should have
been unquestionable song.
Its cumbersome shadow
blots a round of Mozart.
His hands lift from the piano.

The others strung with visible notes
    their lyric loops of light
        and kept the music going on
            about the absent sounds.

But they too stopped
    by the empty site
    and had to drop
one upon one, at the deepening spot,
        and fall with him.

5.

The social world, they said, "drained
Is writing the bringing of justice?   from the work" after
Is just light   the "conventional
justice?   icons of the 30's,"
               the "standard fare
compromised.   of the time." Quote "in
                 1940, when he began
        to spend summers in Martha's Vineyard,
    the social world drained from his work." Unquote.

6.

Narrow market-casting
    is meant to prevent
        feeling much, even any, of this.
    It sutures us to things
we will buy
    whatever, straight thru time
        and never look at shame. The process
has been graduated
    in the dispensary, has been stuffed
        with a fine calibration of insistence.
Ambient desires, flavors, and crunchy patenting of colors
        can tell their demographic riddles
to those with ears to harvest the nuances.

And the autumn wet and drear?
the blood-dark leaf?
the button fallen on the street, some "useless scrap its power"?
The flowering pear that
       went its route, a ruddy green, then full, then red, then gold
then god, then golem-brown, its planet balls of rust that
starlings eat?
          Ghosts. Ghosts of ghosts at the open fosse.

November 1995, February 1996, June–July 1996

Draft 28: Facing Pages

That sense of blockage at the limen
          translating as this word:
               "corruscation"
must have begun with a thing,
          with rust
               or with metal twist, yet
          I can't remember having seen
          anything, in the split second of
                    never known time as such
among the dream. In deep unwake, it
          was given out as having occurred,
                    as being here;
                         whereupon blockage
               emerged directly as a word
          created by dispersals among feeling and shadow.

          Invisible scenes and sounds untraced, where
               I feel the dog now dead nudging my elbow
               to get out, the black
          fur heart mark on her soft white side, or
query a particular puzzle of this tricky site:
          "did my mother die or not?"

          As for "**corruscation**" as a word,
               there are tapping tactics used to
break it into cor, to rus, rust, corridor
               the turns, transposing word parts, double
          facets vocab. and idio. Nuance the unspoken.
                    Not to ignore the relation to "limen"
               as "blocked." Bears a look-see.
          But who actually can bear it?
                    the door resisting entry.
                    the depth defying surface.
                    the shadows telling stories.

The word got spelled with a double "r,"
which was what I first off
took this sign to be:
"corrosion,"
the wearing away, dissolution
gnawed into eaten and eating
by the shadowy baby mirrored back
hinge pivot inside the space. Yet was closer to
"coruscate,"
and indicates flashing, glittering,
senses of light intermittent and vibrant,
misted phosphorescent ground.

This dreamed-out **"corruscation,"**
produces glitter and rust together, transposing each
moment of reading cross the language fonts in that
half-light of coincidence, lush chaos of luck, of lurk the very
twist or strew of "be" and "here";
in the log of the **half-life** —
back from where? the shadowy randomness,
the sort or sors that throws flat down the die;
and in the **third half** lug, with a laugh, third half—
pulling hard between, punching
thru bricked-up spaces, to uncover lintels
for doorways, for doorwas, into which one goes
or thought to step
but tripped the limen
and got caught.

Wild wild wind and wider blow
dark violent sky
trees' greeny heave flags inside out
a twisting quadrant, leaves
turn recto verso, twin and flip the facets
both a wilderness and not, filled and not
dead or not,
the chance of seeing or not,
later finding or not.
The crisp the whispy cast the

crust of language
random twisting
wet direction the tumbling storm
soi-distant
it angels right across the narrow page
dark implacable obsidian
and washes grey green waterthick light
over pre-echoes.

The double face of leaves
leaving across the third.
Second does the first. One is first, one follows.
Then there is a nother. An e rrancy.

Post-storm light flat and coral flood front
over a house
strange in the language
with "intransitive verbs followed by transitive circumstances"
and mini-gestural adjustments of letters
losse for loose
filed for field
think and thing
now and not
those "powerful little berries"
that show that anything could change anything, as we hang here at the
Earthen door
inside readiness.

Speckles the foxglove
among stumps squandered into lumber,
dewy the ragweed over the cumulous waste upbuilt,
rusted out of factories on the urban corridor,
this is the least of it.
"Poem" is nothing in the face of this.
Can not write for a stark seeing, beyond an end point,
a tip point, over that threshold we have tripped,
quasi-baffled, singing out our little song "whoo whee."

Which is how I account for the trouble at the heart of poems.

Hard to mark arousal to a justice deferred,
easy to show a joy sometimes too patent,
that very joy deferring justice
with its own desirable pleasures.

Therefore one can only continue word to word,
word to work, picking thru the vanity of any poem, airy, in
                        day light season time motion cloud
            the circumstances of its composition
                        wherein the lurid boundary of color,
                                the room where it is written
                form, rhetor, lumen
the disturbances of the poet,
                thought that comes unbidden
                                showbread in the tabernacle
                rising as the poem
                                unfolds itself, offering
                the deep and sometimes desperate trouble
                                bred at the heart of poems.

That despite the above wants wwords
wsords LEMON on the page
words' letters, lemen sword
so concrete and intimate, so oil-acrid right
stubbly border where yellow
zest on the cirque
shades to pulp and white.

That because of the above
wants something so "os"
the skeleton of yearning ossuarial, wants
implacable "cold ashes"
placed precisely on the non-dimensional edge
            where underside meets recto/verso,
                        a third space

            made inside the under and through the shift,

            the cusp of facing pages

at the spot between here and there

    between definite poem

    and the wavy registers

        from untranslated sensation,

        untranslatable narratives,

        shadows and their shadow words.

        This is the situation:

        isolate flakes, randomly settled

        ashes that fell being showbread's yeast

        a smudge between here and there

        no one will understand

        this, may be nothing, anyway,

        in the face of it.

                    April–June 1996

Draft 29: Intellectual Autobiography

ck ck ck ck cic
scattered samenesses, in as many
directions: to the sky along the gravel
by the window
through minute
inner slips and other clicks: fast and slow,
light and dark, spectre and color
yes and no

chk, quick
amid disparate axes
dispersing

unsolaced.
        ^
Song of a traveller about to depart.
Song of a returning traveller.
Fancy named warbles, coming and going,
aprobaterion, epibaterion,
whatever.

The gap—a readable
white line of nothing, a drag
weighting the turn—was just lead.

And what happened in that in-between space, was it
technical   kerfluffle   named   rewards   flatness?
Describe your artistic achievement to date.

        "Baffled, I prepare for even greater foreignness."

        ^
Outline the traditions
in which you would place
your work.

Aureate
        dismantling sundry.
Then
        the reverse.

Any Old How
            was the pattern.
(Au petit bonheur
    in francophone.)

Little words,
        worming into incipience.
 "The a."
        Then, half-contrary,
"a the."

            ^

Bilderverbot.
                The moon trapezoid on the cool floor.
        Be that way!   Dreamatis personae.

            ^

Words ending in -ette.
                        Kitchenette.   Dinette.
Luncheonette. Laundromat. Hopper. The cold air,
vedette, that the poem breathes
tries to warm it by "o muse."

            ^

Dora Maar photographed Meret Oppenheim's "Déjeuner en fourrure."
            The saucer cup and spoon pic-nic de fétiche, saucy,
            un grande crème, cum Chinese gazelle
            tropes roughly everything

then, about 23 years after,

"when Yves Klein began to paint with girls instead of brushes"
            a pretty good idea given everything

whole lithe sweep of them,
       the attraction would differ.

Thus
"compelling any writing."
    ^

Briefly locate your current project
and state how you plan
to use your time.

Prix fixe, pixillated
strata of culture to dig
out, mote by mote,
where the strabismic lens of any shard
stops me dead.

Immerginated raptures
       are unsung (so to speak) because the word
       doesn't exist
the word for what we are being led to
in the way of
flattened dialectics
in the articulation of joy despite
and within
the crisis — of burning it all off, the whole earth
ripped out,
the pillar of smoke
visible
as we follow, blankly,
the logic of complexity
in which we were raised.

    ^

Where is the place to stand to say this,
got any syntax would make it clearer?
While we all nickel and dime it
with normal exchanges — are there
       recalibrated tenses

                    for conjugating bafflement in modes
                    tuned to micro-twangy scales of resistance,
          are there ruptured agents
                    for the over-extended job-lost lack-luster
                    X? Anyway
I read some words I wrote, I sound like well-meaning
          translations, just slightly unidiomatic, just off,
by a
kindred foreigner
looking stolidly at the spot
citizen of I-am-not-sure
what.

          ^

"Home, family, illness,
mucus,
childhood,
transitional objects,
household detritus"

thereby

          ^

hearth heart
(h) (h) (h) (h)
my hear
(th) (t) (th) (t)
     ear
     m'ere
     tereu

          ^

Trio midge ant caddis
Luminescence keying
pulse of *the* pleasure
watching *a* registr. ways *it*
suffuses

his jay bounces into the lower branches, thick blue beauty.

^

Will have already
begun to play
long tones
long tones on the saxophone
to hear the overtone series
over and over;
where segments mount and narrow
to follow waveses' vibrating dispersal
to observe reverberations in and of the body,
long tones and overtones
in the long time.

^

Georgics, or Work.

"Work!
work! work!" George yelled
at the aspirant. "You'll have to work
hard
like everyone else."

^

What are your methods? Your response
may be general or specific,
but please limit your comments
to the space provided.

Leaves torn from old notebooks
and mildewed subscription blanks   establishing
on the cut-off margins of newspapers   the mouth(er)-eaten
                                                                                writer.
There are pink scraps, blue and yellow scraps, one of them
a wrapper of Chocolat Meunier
dark bitter, no doubt.
Eat clay cuniform for pica, chew spitballs of paper,

183

snack cartouches
the wilds of stark   SERVING
at the center of the banal   WRIT.

          ^

What are the directions
you plan to pursue in your work?

Nicht mitmachen

There was a second bomb, not to forget it.

During Auschwitz
after Auschwitz
              not enough prepositions and adverbs for this:
nach Auschwitz, to towards in relation to according to
noch Auschwitz, still still still
              for this, and for this.

So chortle under the stark curse
you entitle "Adorno's verse."

          ^

No other world but here.it.is.all.
now.here, all world nowhere
else
the bush, that bush, scarlet
ferocity
flares whenever one catches
sight of this, for
whatever we understand as such
"we are debarred from providing
any indication
whatsoever

that we are inconsolable."

^

Given, as well, attacks on positions of opening
                           orphic trek back pack little speck

            exposed on that escarpment

Pneunomena

of the status que, we are object cases

in "real time." What looked like a Bad Register

in print.   our lives smudged.   off-ink.   blurred.   caught wrong.

we had wanted more hope.

   ^

Where
"it literally rains little songbirds"
warblers, orioles, tanagers, flycatchers and thrushes
drained is to become a golf course
specially written into a House bill

   ^

Wet snow clumped
words, clumped and melted
lacy pivot points with ice dipped into the
strange cold heat of praxis,
in a white wet storm, and ruffles up its dark
truncated rigging—
some coracle, some jot on wheels
rolls the present through the potlatch
humming its way along
a single spot of ground
into a sinking patch of time.

   ^

Propose a work, the work, a work of enormous dailiness, vagrant
responses inside the grief of a century. Pain, of suspicion, of care, the
deformative, washing and cutting that occur
dilatory, minute
in cataclysm, can't help it.   The small time.
Propose
staring at all you know some of it, what cannot be represented
per se
but just exists, in the backwash of gesture
forgotten,

that is forgotten every day

without, and within, memory.

December 1995, June–July 1996

Draft XXX: Fosse

Imagine a book, a little book,
    whose words are covered
        one by one
with the smallest pebbles—
        fossils imprinted, shale splinters,
slag and gnarls from fossick,
        cheap sweepings arrayed,
a road of morse lines
    step by step
        down the page.

It looks like poetry, runs along depths
    on the surface, slugs
        of a text that is lost;
the instruction it offers
    is delicate,
        maybe misplaced.

The words and their syntax
    come
        not to nothing
        (for the lover of pebbles)
but to an irradiating splayed out
    Something
        so large
it can only be
    marked thus:

+ It could say erosion of the book.

    The pace of the traveller
slowed along the Hansel-Gretel highway,
    given bits of scrap and cornbread
that innocent birds go after, given shiny pebbles
    far too pretty for the story.

The easy exit does not exist.
The circumstance offers more.
She had laid that trail to have it get effaced,
in order to be abandoned
to the scrub of a dark wood.

+ It says erasure so cunningly,
mimics little words
(flat pebbles),
brings them all to the *a*
or to the *the* of "be."
Can choose to investigate.

+ The wordless words
behind the blocked out words
can be more compassionate than
the word.
The pebbled lines are filled with otherness;
With only the speech of the stone,
they gain in empathy.
Reopen pity.

+ Deep ditch, road cut, folds of rock
propose a book of the unraveling voice
incapable and swamped
in the same time as the self.

There is a modulation of feeling
"set myself this meditation"

impossible

project

barely   { ready
            { reading

to begin.

•

Imagine a reader, who would resist
        and not resist—
Lightning flashes
        hot silverline domes over the mountain—

resist each word
        even the long night of characters, actions, choreography
which reenact her plundering defiance, resist
        and still articulate the gloss,
        the implacable sweetness
of the Stone.

Narrative sections contain instruction, include
statements about underpass and loophole
do this, do that, listen, do not
disobey,
invest yourself beyond yourself
for you are
a representative of fire
in the windy hopeless cavern, a spark
unable to warm the dark but able still
to see its flaring cries

even
without light, able
to clasp the mists of loss.

There is a space, a ditch
        shallow along the contours of earth
                this bumpy knoll or that hillock
but deep enough to cover
        whatever
                for a couple of years,
until it worms out
        its readable shard,
                its hoops of unforgiveable bone.

Here to imagine the reader
marked by another ring of mark a / a \

makr, all that morganlongne daag dawning, of
the mist
the missed

for a meniscus tension of exhumation
swells the page—

fugue and segue, modicums of $\begin{cases}\text{wonder}\\\text{wander}\end{cases}$
for the $\begin{cases}\text{locus}\\\text{logos}\end{cases}$

all along the shifting $\begin{cases}\text{boundary}\\\text{bounty}\end{cases}$

·

Childrenhad gottenup to the attic
hadtaken the boxedmemor
abilia and begunto strew
discovery
    the past became
clutter upon clutter.
   There was no order, no size, no year;
      emotional response was totally mixed.
        What turned up,
what had gone, where by accident something
     was into another box. . . . And the book
   of photographs no longer
     fits here, once it was looked at,
        thereupon put, or push, or pull it into, or
out of there. Thus the random recovery
   of unresolved tidbits
can never be assimilated.
    This is the condition of time, going forward athwart
no matter the "gifts" of shame, fantasy, and memory,
   no matter the organic strangeness
of irreversibility.
    This is the condition of time

stuck all over (Merzhouses of Tyree Guyton in Detroit)
with debris of
temporalities gone
            (Merzhouses of Tyree Guyton bulldozed)
        nothing and everything
        plaster-faced dolls,
        plastic tops from margerine tubs,
        tin tea trunk

outcrop

along strata of ever-disjunctive

                folds, and smash.

                                            •

Imagine it
        without the rhetorics of pity
            but not pitiless,
O ruisseaux, O bull of gold and
        lapis, the tongue
            blue lapis
thick with lyric and wine,
        caught in bosky lute trees
caught for song, for song;
        the charm that licks your ear,
Bos Voice
        webbed one way round with strings
            and wound by
linen and pegs. To hold.
        Pressured against. The wood
and sinews gut bound
        leaned into the plectrum
like a figurehead
        drenched by rose.

The bull plays within himself
        at the heart of the labyrinth.

Can visit him dead
bask in his anger and the dirty light
of poetry
and try it all again
astir, that
trenchant call across the fosse
to activate
something
        is it prophecy?
        is it instruction?
        is it mourning?

Whatever the genre,

let it "pass thru its own answerlessness."

           ·

      Go stony book

      Step across

      Embrace the wraithe

not as demanded in foundational commandment

nor as refused in annihilating compleynt

but just in the course of things

casting oneself to the same winds.

                          June–July 1996

Draft 31: Serving Writ

Given
    that the work undertaken to date
      glosses two words: IT and IS
and sets nomads a-wander
    thru and fro this site
      graven with rivulets of marking;
Given
    that "the common air includes
      Events listening to their own tremors,"
them in "unassuaged unrest" at the prospect
    of "adding another edge to the page" —
      even a hairline crack
articulated from seepage and stipple
    "disquieting in its shadow
      and its rage";
Given
    its joy; right, given Joy:
      Go flash pink swells
Go "gold sweat" high and blinding
    where crows work over the last at last,
      eh-eh-eh-eh ah ah eh-eh-eh-eh
exacting number codes of 2 and 4
    they do, and lurk over the lintels of every door
      that opens on the filiated Here,
Beech, Dog, Loggia, Pitcher, Vertigo
    thereby Hear — every unspeakable untellable
      X, its pluck and jube,
    its incalculable harmonics toll.

Given all this, there is nothing but this to say.
    The work has exceeded its original memory.

October–November 1996

Draft 32: Renga

Snarled light, snap, bare.
      Of golden glass light trees, of Knots
              to which one is apprenticed,
        of split splints intransigent,
                 no beginning beginning.

::

    no beginning but
    emptiness full, fulling
    in-betweens.

What twisting ribbon (time? or light? or words?) is

it Aglows Astripe?

::

That glows, stripes and

branches, while bursts

of gold-glass light snarls

complicate

"the tangle of it."

::

The tangle-basket's
           split stone lid
rests on plaited shims of bark —

Brush twist total. The words' single streamer makes

boundaries from overlays, from twigs and space.

::

Borders and overlays between twigs and space

                               Small reds and Slight greenings.

Sideshadows, caught arrays of them
there were, and darkling crossbeams

through which—

::

Through which (come)
night-rems and day-vectors
plumy and plummy blues.
This (thus) can (n)ever
register "it" enough.

::

Can never register it enough,

its cross-greens, purple croci or cerulean squill,

its (g)utterals or (c)harms—

these watery buds, its fingers in orfi that

awaken manifolds.

::

Manifolds awake,

wrestle, rustle the restlessness of it

"the back and forth of early sounds, small cries,"
                    the "little owl of the waste places"

fat squat that robin.

::

Fat and squint that robin's
rufous flair, parking-lights white,
that lands into a dapple scattered on the feathery field,
marches around.
One plot.

::

Subplot. They are always saying—

can you write this story? you're a writer.

What story?

o world whirr were or was

Children, pretending birds, yell CHIRP.

::

Kids flap birds, Whirrr chirrr wheerr T
with merle noir warble, rouge gorge warble,
wobble, braiding these sounds
with
tiny dissonant ones.

::

Tiny dissonant plaited
irritants

hint at self-similar melodies
that chain from leaf-bare trees,
meshed trees, pip-bar was where?

::

meshed trees (w)here

woodpeckers nab the births of slugs and bugs

(w)here words as words
        from the diction-laden (g)round
                pass beyond words.

::

To pass beyond words
yet construct linkage,s meaning,s in unspoken space.
                For still it's reasonable / Reasonable is it?

                        that

dark lines, inexplicable in every force and fusion, intersect.

::

"the dark lines which negate them and intersect

too tentative, the figures too small:

but this is the point: the work is its tentative-

ness, its smallness, its off-ness, what

some may call lack."

::

lack, lack in each fragment

Call the smallness minority
or luck. Whatever   Little-
        ness -ness
                from dark and hidden lines.
::

Dark line, hidden, limns
        young crescent sliver round its own curbed orb:
                in truth, a dark light,
                        the one to come
                        the one before.

::

Whether it's one before
or one to come—
"little" is odd, the 5-odd inching hand
at the horizon holds "us" as we are.
Someone standing out in the night.

::

Stands still under the hemisphere of night

estimating arc'd degrees from the horizon

to see Hale–Bopp, 40 million mile tail,

take up one iota of the sky

an inch or two to the eye.

::

An inch or two to the eye
spinning and streak at the lee of a dome,
or what we see as such: our pitchblack shining—
scale, word, concept, call.

Opening yod, the book is awake.

::

Opening the yod that goes with this space
the book is awake

enters a tiny point.
The-point.
of the-The

.

::

The-the. A-the.
What a book!
Presenting streaks in light
of celestial smoke
by folding black A's inside white the's.

::

Black ABC's code inside
this white fold, that little slip

frill and sweet honey ruffle
multiple registers that travel
to the serif of one letter.

::

The serif of one letter or

one red dot
dripping a flower-fashioned fractal
over the peony core.
Then at edges, everything's midrash.

::

Right at the edge, midrash piled on midrash, Pelion on Ossa, to

highlite the vitreous floaters with comment and interp. And there's

     the "yesterday I"
               had a diaristic impulse but

       it didn't work out, now, did it?

::

or Did it? Can't tell? Blame

the unwritable oddities of journey — "the daily";

blame the persistent bad manners of the dark horse

mashing the other one in the yoke,

bumping sideways into — o that horse! — the gloss.

::

The gloss also comes bumping and travelling sideways

full of "enjabments" that doth
make the poem show as such
     it gives a little poke
     "watch me go under"

::

     "watch me go under"

mossy flip dunking
bell-note;
stone plump, plunk.

     "watch me stay under"

::

under or blunder?

memorized or mesmerized?

oculist or occultist?   } Your Call

annotated or anointed?

::

Call und risposto.
See Strange-Handed Puella
            endowed with the letter
    "little i inside the whole alphabet"
            loop the cardinal swizzle toy around her head.

::

Head of the I-loop
            how many
functions of memory, of noticing, of awe, of loss to
be (,) Endowed with some letters (time and pressure)
            does poetry (,) remember?

::

And Does she remember

the photo as it was taken
        does she remember seeing ex post facto the album
        does she know that girl she sees

        does she know the oddity

::

To know the astonishing oddity
   of the long-gone as if
      it could be stored

      what use is memory forgetting is overwhelming

      shapes fade at the limen crossover
::

Shapes at the limen, crossing
      cardinal turbulence, bosco, name, pitcher, vertigo
      projecting future memory, Monte Acuto, open window
      (Italy?)
where ride the random biddyings and cars.

::
      Of random air sounds, coo and biddy, here is something,
      some main clause
the language laddered in mystery
wrestling with an angel who claims "he" ("it"?)
is memory.

::

memory, is
something scat that sings Yo moon
orphan si wah bo wap truuit,
a-labile

lag.

::

A lag, after the blizzard

Large low moon rise, pink and wide, but
at the very moment of eclipse
loss of the moon to snow clouds.
No show: March 24, 1997.

::

March 25, 1997, daffs fall flat

neck green snaps an inch

beyond the perianth
loss, but not irrevocable.
Trace into place.

::

Trace into place, just by one chance, not another—
cross-hatched weaves
with runs, buzzes and diddles of oddities
throughout the microclimate

       that, minute, wavers right here.

::

Minute wavers right here:

frost was "candied vapor"
hail was "broken water"
snow was "curdled water"

it was all like that. That time, like that place.

::

It was, like,
impending harbingers were, "like that's some."
Space and waywardness
in a handful
of wet dust.

::

There's a handful of wet dust
that is detted you, a gift,
debt you, due you, that you do
whose instruction even when resisted
          is irresistible.

::

          Irresistible
                    the pinhole chance
generating just that wonder
of human shadow over the implacable.

Hard not to take the call—

::

Hard to refuse the call. But Q.:

"what happens when the daughter of Mnemosyne
has not received the gift
of narration?"

Ans.: This (?).

::

This answers to what exactly?

"These are just examples
          of how she subdues the unpredictable"

It's true—Subdues, or Survives—

          seeing it in different lights.

::

Look at it in this light.

204

Imprint of the bare trees stand as
neither line exactly nor curve, not *i* nor *s,* but as particular cases—
sun, wind, openness, whatever
they turn and come to makes the next—

::

Particular cases of turning, next creates next,

"is" *is* action; memory a mode of thought

scumbled on a neural surface

that struggles with attachment

inside and despite fragment.

::

Attachment inside and despite fragment:

pinholes of entry, broad strangeness, twisted joist,

and snarls of light on the floor.

Been there. Done that.

Words, anyway, are "fuzzy sets."

::

In words made of words' fuzziness and interlock,

"The 'it' is not identified in this sentence,"

it drifts laterally

inside, and of space, "site of watchfulness"

moves through its own thickness and thinness.

::

Thickness thinness
     thisness thatness
grain by grain as the mist, as clay or humus,

as cold starfire, as depth magnetism, its

-idity.

::

idity; burr-ditty,
    more scat and doggerel

can zing those descriptors,
    whether they're done in "viewless pencil" or low-res pixel,

     for rogueish maps or for symmetrical immersions.

::

If it's Immersive Symmetries
vs. "unassuaged unrest":

go instability.

The symmetries don't bear watching

only the restless stragglers, the incident off.

::

Only the strugglers (stragglers) looking across

a territory to which they (technically) belong yet
are homeless, and therefore speak in parable and renga,
of angles, of the sky, and of details, of letters and of commands
unfathomable : flat, spiky, dotted as scrub.

::

Flat dotted with scrub.
Calls irrevocable in an intransigent wilderness.
Someone
          Crossing thru this micro-space
                    Loosened the trail pebbles.

::

The loosened quirky pebbles
          Changed position
                    leaving molds and holes crusty
                    jagged And settled with
The slightest shift. New outlines, not that different.

::

Not that different, but different enough.

I stare with the deep-filled eye of the past
along the unrecoverable border called "my life," "today"
or "now"
where any detail becomes a limen.

::

There are limens one cannot go back on,

memory isn't always memory
info after: did I remember
or did I remember remembering?

I was wordless, sleepless.

::

"I, wordless, tried sleeping, but couldn't"

all the loss imbedded on this pallet

reaching a point and an enormity

 of nothing

I am

::

I am

just walking to and f—

Not one day, not one night
goes by
that it is not before you.

::

It is before you
    "world's dusky brink"
in the flickering light
    held in the little

paper for writing or the small screen.

::

The paper for writing or the light screen
        dip at the touch
of words, a sip ladled
        from a bucket of sadness
                where the well is unnameable.

::

An unnameable well of writing done on gold
      with silver, paper the gold
          crinkles letters of silver
      the foils of one over the other
          into the fosse-filled debris.

::

      Fossick — search the waste piles,
the washings,
      of their names for gold
their golden names

 that want a witness.

::
      Wanting to witness

wants to wander, to speak more

small than fog, to speak so small
as to be perfectly
mute.

::

Perfectly mute, of mountain fog and sea smoke

we cannot see ourselves

but we breathe the ways of turbulent fluids

in the physical landscape of homelessness

Open the door

::

Open the door
a weeper was pleading
to a stone room,
so chary, that took the path
of the indifferent.

::

Don't be indifferent
she so old and mis-wired
she said "you put a dybbuk in the house"
did I? I didn't? I didn't care.
Translucence was what I thought about, then.

::

He had said Translucence
was about the only thing he
wanted (his medium, porcelain)

and time, and I? Can I acknowledge
my answer?

::

I answered *here am I*
and *there I am*:
  and this makes doubling, an overlay in time

    and snarls the translucence

  by desires for the clutter, the debris, the broken.

::

  Wanting the clutter and debris, the broken

  seam, the jagged mend,
    the scar with its tiny stitches

patched, and then reclawed;
sad and ferocious —

::

Ferocious lost words
in the very dawn
of motive
        take this child, and spring struggle
rip of silvery bud packs

::

rip of silvery bud packs

pink tree blood tinging the green
chartreuse bubble of the maple

that every year "the little fingers of the oak"
curl a tiny hair of hope

::

Hairbreadth hope of the leaf curls
green wedging (out of the lustrous bark)
green drooping (out of the brown casings)

such mercy mire me — foliage
and three-sided light

::

With nothing to look at but light's
three sides come suffusing

around the blanket, was that a windowframe or edge of a nose?
oddities

of reading the ways light enters space

::

Reading ways light enters space

   the moon so misted
  looks eclipsed,

bright folds
over the detail.

::

Details match along the fold
hum and bong
one can dwell there, or is this *here*?
one can resist, can even
blow into the instrument

::

The way he blows into the instrument's

tubing, the clarinet arterial

to make blooping turns of direction

to go out sonorous and

tuneless, timeless into time

::

Timed half-tuneless modulations, without the mouthpiece

music woosh in the tunnel of the head
as if an echo the intransigence of space
unruly
fro and true

::

The to and fro of the one trek
hunching under the keystone of that story
the whole constructed as a trap and revelation
the key in the lock turns tighter
bound to its premise, the keyhole

::

Keyhole of titmice spread their tails
soft pink belly
exposed and jumping to the other
flash of their sexuality

       spaces between as they cry and play

::

spaces of the field, the cry, the play,
spaces of the dot stars or crumbs narrowly

imposs
       impass

of blue eyed grasses spikey potes own power

::

       deep blue winks sweetgrass
in which low down eyebright

         grounds eyelight splintered
         thin white-blue with dark blue lines up

such raggedy performances of words

::

of words in rags

such as "moonlight"
or "small apple bite" (green)
shift your eyes, for a second and they're lost, just streaks
down the page, and they all become foreign, even the simplest.

::

Yet the simplest also return, at odd moments
Flecks of the past
thinking of their house now
and shame of an event there

just remembering their name

::

Just remembering their last name

upended stories glistening with balladry

the stark single detail—father over son—

the force of one thing

invested beyond happiness or sadness.

::

"Today you may remember
        the happiness of last week.

Tomorrow you may remember
        why you were happy.

The story comes in pieces."

::

Coming in pieces. Not even a story.
A dot of Red 2 to work into the white margarine
White fur chair with the burn circle deep in the arm

merry, the storm monochromatic

now the wandering.

::

Wander looketh up,
the trees have leaves, when did that happen (?)

beech leaves out of crisp rust-colored packets
the oak and its looping golden flowers
the soft back silver and the delicate greening.

::

Bright green of new leaves and large green light blowing
showing spaces inside words,

silver impossible words cannot do it; it is a space

creating a change of scope

scales get blasted

::

Scale—like one inch to a mile/ to test us

even the most banal relationship/ is odd:

what does a "map" mean/ can one credit

a here/ slightly off center from the last

stroke.

::

a Here up and off center,

flying over a blank and snow-filled plain
in which three clear mountains exist
the wide site of event
one and two and three

::

one and two and three

three kinds of slippage: ridge, peak, volcano
        a kind of renga chain
is what we live on;
        it cannot help be odd.

::

It is so odd, it is so curious.

A gigantic spherical object at the deep center of earth:
under the crust, slower than the surface,
heavier than the moon and nearly as large as it
revolves round and round beneath our feet.

::

Under our feet, after the hail

salads of torn leaves cover the streets.

Ground between two stones, two moons, and a comet

we blow like wheat and chaff together

through the air of our stepping.

::

Stepping into
"inevitability," journey that is "the binding,"
"I have been wading a very long river"
sloshing across waywardly
trying not to go too quickly.

::

Go
quickly.
No
summary.
Touch that knife.

::

    In time, the infinite,
the knife
comes down; it's
an angel
holds the point.

::

Holds the deep point,

tipped against one edel finger,

the blade dulls

in that kind light.

But if said angel did not catch the brunt in time?

::

Catching the brunt of time

given the memory of the site
should we be grateful or angry?
Glad to submit, or glad to be spared it?

There is ladder and chain, binding and knife.

::

Ladder, chain and binding:
Light snarls around the walkers.
These paths are dusty, people thirsty.

The point is—not to question what you are given;
The knife is, you can't help it.

January 1997–August 1997

Draft 33: Deixis

for Robin Blaser
"It gives it its authority." [1]

Like translations, poems
        say the unsayable twice,
                once to another language.
Speak to each other
Twice thru another,
        yet once in one again,
                say bits of conjunction, fragments of mark.

But why did you cut
        the "little porch"
                translating that poem
as if the poet hadn't put
        it there.
                Then changed the change.
No one will know
        The loss was lost
                Now left no mark.

When is that now
right now?
What twisting ribbon
of time, of light, of words?

It's "Now"
        full-empty,
                and site specific
because anyone and everyone
        lives poised there,
                put, so to speak, in its place.

---

1. "It gives it its authority." Wlad Godzich, "Foreword" to Paul de Man, *The Resistance to Theory*. (Minneapolis: University of Minnesota Press, 1986), p. xv. Translation: Deixis gives theory its authority. Does this term authority mean the authority of deixis to articulate the distinctions between there and here, of reference shifting? Or is it the authority of theory to articulate specificity, to point? The etymology of "deixis" means to point.

Say "I." Say "here."
　　Say "now," "then,"
　　　　"recently," "soon," "today." [2]

We seem to behold only
　　a small part
　　　　of an infinitely extended structure.
　　Yet its small space I can hardly name.

Why in that poem
　　did he miss the ledge or edge
　　　　on which the chronic bird
was come to stand—
　　charged to tell us
　　　　when now becomes then.

Was it cut, or was it
　　leap to another line,
　　　　over the place in time

which falls out
　　black motes
　　　　blown letter-like from page.

Maybe "porticina" turned
　　in its Am.Lang situation
　　　　to kitsch

one It. detail too many
　　given cuckoo bird
　　　　and striking from,

given
　　"someone forgot to adjust the pendulum"

---

2. This list of words from John Lyons. And this definition: "By deixis is meant the location and identification of persons, objects, events, processes and activities being talked about, or referred to, in relation to the spatiotemporal context created and sustained by the act of utterance and the participation in it, typically of a single speaker and at least one addressee." John Lyons, *Semantics: 2* (Cambridge: Cambridge University Press., 1977), p. 637. I am grateful to Muffy Siegel for this reference.

so time was ticking much too fast
    in this brown chalet with its little porch
      on which bird was

ours to
    step, with
      its comic sound of hours
      the unsayable.

The spot of pressured time
writing for love, in haste
what one wanted done is not.
Or perhaps it was just passed over,
in simple error. Random.

Is it that Words are Waste?
Will sheer pointing
save the place?
    Cannot be.
    For 'twas also a dream,
to show, shining

    wordless, pointing to
pierce thru absolutes of here,

how the present
    becomes historical.

What, then, is the size of the loss?
A little word, one word or another
here or there?
And now it's put back?
It's hardly lack, but is
the incessant waver of words.
Wager of words, words thick and mere.
Symbolical. What happens everywhere.

For any (instantiated) flick of time
    is fated

        to be, in an instant,
    the there of distance.

And all its fullness, whatever we had felt
       at any time,
          is gone,
all the
       textures and overlays
that even at the time we could not fully feel
maybe not share
indeed had repressed many or most of what it was
       all those that's
       are now
beyond unrecoverable.

       Therefore
Deixis is a strange flare.
       For all its terms,
like here and there, or
       you and I
depend
       on the door opening and a
tolling sound
       between the unspoken
and the disappearance

of where we are: is this *there* sunny sweet
       or grey, changeable, ablow?
How do we understand: it's raining?
Is it?
It is just air.

Thus deixis evokes the sited words of poetry.
Silent moments
       blank then filling with
          something
with the next
       pulse
       of

"relational valence
or vectorial give and take."[3]

Of it, speaking awkwardly
in the convergence of quirks.

So Now is a Night preserved
in yet another space, in space that's
neither Night nor Now.[4]

It is a site where language hangs
over itself vertiginous

and locks
(did you expect lacks? or luck?
did you want leaks? or loot?)

where the key fits to a door in the middle of nowhere
(now here)
and turns itself, like a riddle.

This is the deictic click
opens the corridor down which words
travel their wandering annals,
bunched in metamorphic pleats
not homage to Ovid, but Benveniste

"positing another who, being
completely exterior to 'me'"

---

3. Nathaniel Mackey, "Sound and Sentiment, Sound and Symbol," in
The Politics of Poetic Form: Poetry and Public Policy, ed. Charles Bern-
stein (New York: Roof Books, 1990), p. 88.

4. Hegel's *Phenomenology of Spirit*,"To the question: 'What is Now?' let
us answer, e.g. 'Now is Night.' In order to test the truth of this sense-cer-
tainty a simple experiment will suffice. We write down this truth; a truth
cannot lose anything by being written down, any more than it can lose
anything through our preserving it. [sic; one might question both
thoughts] If now, this noon, we look again at the written truth we shall
have to say that it has become empty. The Now that is Night is pre-
served." The passage goes on; as cited by Giorgio Agamben, *Language
and Death: The Place of Negativity,* trans. Karen Pinkus with Michael
Hardt (Minneapolis: University of Minnesota Press, 1991), p.10.

becomes an echo
"becomes my echo
to whom I say *you*
and who says *you* to me."[5]

How can we credit that "you" just echoes me?

Odd that to
live in the deictic space
of exchange and positionality
gets so tricky
that here one of its theoretic masters
posits you-
      being-
Echo, which is
impossible since even when you say
    you after my *you*, you are
surely not echoing
        my Narcissus
    but have one of your own.
    Have one in your now.

This image of owlish other
      going you-you-you
blocks consideration of a
    personable you
    disturbs the exchanges and imbalances
    moving between us,
    o really endless you,

seasoned by when. And in our shredded texture.
Perhaps he means "ecco."
"Becomes my 'ecco'"

straight only as a perpetual, mobile, continuously moving
road, or way, between these points
    that shift
        when I listens and you speaks.

---

5. Emil Benveniste, "Subjectivity in Language," *Problems in General Lin-guistics* (1966). Translated by Mary Elizabeth Meek (Coral Gables: University of Miami Press, 1971), p. 225.

Speaking anyhow,
　　　as Blaser remarks,
inside the little "I" which
　　　"is neither first,
　　　　　　nor a person,
　　　nor singular"
　　　such an "I" could address itself as "you"
　　　self-divided, familiar as a spirit,

　　　the "je" who ate that outre,
　　　deep other inside the heart of the place
　　　revenant
　　　shadows and their shadow words.

　　　It is especially "that."
　　　What did you say?
　　　I didn't hear

everyone tacking here and there
where the door swings on its double-jointed hinge
and shakes those cubes of chance
the rooms
in which we toll. [6]

Deixis as the pointing
　　　moment of "the the"
　　　　　(trans. that that), [7]

6. Robin Blaser, *The Holy Forest* (Toronto: Coach House Press, 1993), pp. 317–318.

7. Wallace Stevens, "Man on the Dump," *The Collected Poems of Wallace Stevens* (NY: Knopf, 1957), p. 203. Muffy Siegel pointed out that "the" is not deictic: instead that / this is—demonstrative pronouns and adjectives. It is hard to give up that "that" buried in this emphatic citation from Stevens, so I won't, but, as I suggested, one should think of it as "that that" for perfect accuracy. (See Lyons 654: "There is historical support for the view that the definite article results from the phonological reduction of the unstressed forms of what is diachronically identifiable with 'that' in certain positions.") A statement by Louis Zukofsky offers the poetics of this kind of examination of the smallest words that might, at times, be the words of the deictic: "The poet wonders why so many today have raised up the word 'myth,' finding the lack of so-called 'myths' in our time a crisis the poet must overcome or die from, as it were, having become too radioactive, when instead a case can be made out for the poet giving some of his life to the use of the words *the* and *a*: both of which are weighted

puzzle of "What it is is it."[8]
    ecstasy of "that they are there!"[9]
perfection of
    "Here I/ am. There/ you are,"[10]
double dutch step "Here/This/There/That"[11]
and many swinging more
    "these subtle forays
into the gauche infrastructures
    of movement"[12]
by the edge of open
    deep in instances of discourse[13]
down derry down.

---

with as much epos and historical destiny as one man can perhaps resolve. Those who do not believe this are too sure that the little words mean nothing among so many other words." "Poetry for my Son when he can Read" (1946), *Prepositions* (London: Rapp & Carroll, 1967), p. 18.

8. Lyn Hejinian, *My Life* (Los Angeles: Sun & Moon Press, 1987), p. 82. Also André Bréton in the "Manifesto of Surrealism" (1924) when he remarks that the characters in the "false novels" surrealism aspires to write "will conduct themselves with the same ease with respect to active verbs as does the impersonal pronoun 'it' with respect to words such as 'is raining,' 'is,' 'must,' etc." It is the word for shifts of location: you/I as I/you. Breton, "Manifesto of Surrealism" (1924), translated by Richard Seaver and Helen R. Lane, in Breton, *Manifestoes of Surrealism* (Ann Arbor: University of Michigan Press, 1969), p. 31.

9. George Oppen, *Collected Poems* (New York: New Directions, 1975), p. 78.

10. Robert Creeley, *The Collected Poems of Robert Creeley, 1945–1975* (Berkeley: University of California Press, 1982), p. 389.

11. Ann Lauterbach, *On a Stair* (New York: Penguin Books, 1997), p. 70.

12. Max Kozloff, *Photography and Fascination: Essays* (Danbury, NH: Addison House, 1979), p. 8.

13. "What is the 'reality' to which I or you refers? Only a 'reality of discourse' that is something quite singular. . . . There is no point in defining these terms and demonstratives in general through deixis . . . if we do not add that deixis is contemporaneous with the instance of discourse that bears the indication of the person; from this reference the demonstrative derives its unique and particular character. . . ." Benveniste vol. 1, 252–253, cited in Agamben, 23–24. Agamben goes on to say that "pronouns . . . are presented as 'empty signs,' which become 'full' as soon as the speaker assumes them in an instance of discourse." (Agamben, 24)

My particular forays
　　　　are made of words, arraged
by segmentivity along the line of anguage.[14]
　　　　I mean anguish and anger, mean
the loss of L—
　　　　down to the very bone of oss,
the stone I put my head upon
　　　　taking such rock for pillow.

This is done by a method of the detail,
of the dot, the dit, the dite and dight
the surd of word
a caught schwa within underglot
some particulars of crot
singing, singeing the bitty signs, sighs
breathing up ashen white fire.

The book's black
　　　　　　fire shimmered;
　　　　　　and each
　　　　　　shredded serif
　　　　a-swirl from darker fumes of the past
　　　　　　blew
　　　　through the wind tunnel of hypnogogery.

My first poem was "Memory."
A take on here and there, a step, another, up
231st St. hill, cigarette billboard, a waste
edge, daisy asters and leggy ragweed.
I stop, I stopped, I continue to stop
　　　　here (that is, there) to consider step,
　　　　　　　to see
the shadow form of place
　　　　where I had been
　　　　　　the shadowy form of me.
Therefore I understood myself
　　　　speaking
　　　　　　into watchfulness

---

14. Rachel Blau DuPlessis, "Manifests," *Diacritics* 26, 3/4 (Fall/Winter
1996): 31–53.

a space not of the self
        but of a void that exists as such.

All my next poems were,
        you might say, also
entitled Memory
yet my memory was left in a ravine.

I rejected to portray,
        to memorialize,
                to sing that ruffled lay
that poems essay
—I was no daughter of
unpronounceable Mnemosyne—

        and being the woman writing, anyway,
        Master of the Female Half-Lengths
        I was ambivalent in re:
        the beautiful and its "dove-grey." [15]

Thus doggedly
I clopped away
from memory, muted its X'd ray
by half-measures going halfway.

What was this Memory of?
        It was years.

Five elements four gates, rhumbic directions
        a bright bell-noise
                the color of colors
desire not for the fixed object
but for a melting down, and building up again
incessant the universe of form
even in the smallest room

---

15. Pound speaks against the "viewy" and the "dove-grey" in "A Retrospect" (1913–1918), *The Literary Essays of Ezra Pound*, ed. T. S. Eliot (London: Faber & Faber, 1954), p. 7 and 5. Of course, many of his modernist criteria (hard, "no emotional slither") are implicitly antifeminine, despite originating in praise of H.D.

tapping colors over a template
then with a hand, a sandstorm
sweeping the once formed grains back over the finished form
    to make the formless

until finish is cast away.[16]
It was all luminous and/or all destroyed.
I had to learn that it was Memory of the void.

"It" was immediately constituted
as a topic.
Right away, the word "fold"
was used.
One can dwell here, or is this
"there"?
"I am trying to describe
    the foreignness,
        the outsideness"[17]
    of being inside the site,
        at the same time
            far from it.
There is a shift from silence to writing.
    One feels as if the white page
        a gleam of light, adequate to itself
        with brightness, such positive brightness

constructs a demonstration
    of access to a larger site
        where fold becomes void, and void is fold.

A measure of what we do not know
        a reminder of intricacies that cross our paths,
        a hinge, turning outward and inward, like a page,
    a little spot to stand.

---

16. A Kalachakra Mandala, made as a particle mandala, a temporary arrangement of bits of colored material such as grains of sand or flower petals, was constructed (though not completed in the time allotted) by Lobsang Samten at Swarthmore College, for a week in September 1997.

17. Robin Blaser, "The Fire," in *Poetics of the New American Poetry*, ed. Donald Allen and Warren Tallman (New York: Grove Press, 1973), p. 243.

Here is the time for the thing called the sayable
here its tiny home
here as exchange is its unsayable.

And here is the oddity: that
I is not speaking to *you* but to *it*
   (For the poet I, is speaking
and it to I,
   (to it, and it
the shift between them
   (to I; shifting
brings I to the status of it.
   (brings I to it like a gift.

PN 228.[18] On my knees
between metaphor and translation
say I fell. It isn't true
and plot like that,
the plotzy sentiment, I resist;
so, wait, let's say I didn't fall, I'd knelt.
Heavy, this penumbra of declaration.
So say myself went looking for
some call number
that happened to be on the lowest shelf.

In the old story it was clear who called,
   but in this-now can only stamp the thing "answered"
   and maybe falsify date of receipt.
So to the call, I called back *here am I*
and *there I am*:

   I mean, there is no
I here now
to hear or speak or know,
I am there,
to (maybe two)
speak out of the it

---

18. I see my book, misshelved; *Writing Beyond the Ending* is PS 228.

speak out It. [19]
Let It speak
Make it know and no. Now.
Make It (what) Knew.

Flanged with prosody
bolted to or from or onto
the dead

over a gravel and rutted road
this is a poetry where one feels the road under
the feel
the feet
climb

thru the darkness of this dark
face of poems not written
waste of time not taken
taste of travels somber
and the problem is
how to make poetry

not remembering

but constructed of Memory
time going forward athwart,
a here and a not here
textured, unexpected, flashing, erased,
alive in the flip of the void—
the problem
is how to make poetry
constructed of It.

---

19. See this from Robert Duncan: "The play of first person, second person, third person, of masculine and feminine and neuter, the 'it' that plays a major role in recent work, is noticeably active in the multiphasic proposition of voice in my poetry, where impersonations, personifications, transpersonations and depersonation, again from the earliest levels of development in my language are always at play." Robert Duncan, "The Self in Postmodern Poetry," in *Fictive Certainties* (New York: New Directions, 1985), p. 220.

Memory has meaning
    as an instance of discourse
        it is an activity
that fills and empties like a shifter.

It calls up a spot between the recto/ verso
somewhere along the knife of the page.

Spot neither the oft-spoken, nor the unspoken, but the
in-between

the place of the change.[20]

Someone said "Deixis
    is the linguistic mechanism"
        articulating the distinctions

"between the here and the there,
    the now and the then,
        the we and the you."

"It establishes the existence
    of an 'out there' that is not
        an 'over here,'
and thus it is fundamental to the theoretical enterprise."[21]

---

20. Benveniste (221–222) calls the I–you relation "instances of discourse." But in poetry, it seems to me that two conditions are true that "The Nature of Pronouns" excludes. First, although for Benveniste, the "third person" is "never being reflective of the instance of discourse" (never, that is, in an intersubjective relation with I, such as I–you), I would insist, and have "argued" here, that in the moment of specific poetic discourse, there is exchange between the I and it. Second, the third person is "not being compatible with the paradigm of referential terms like here, now" (while I would want to argue that *it* speaks in and through the now, perhaps just as it flicks into the then).

21. A citation from Wlad Godzich, "Foreword" to Paul de Man, *The Resistance to Theory*. Interesting that while Benveniste emphasizes "intersubjectivity" and the terrain of exchange between the I and the you, Godzich emphasizes the distinctions between the units.

Who would deny this,
given *it* and given *is*,
given that "location of
the participants" matters.[22]
     But it appears oddly harsh,
and also somewhat
          automatic, drawing
such an unwavering line between the elements,
         for in poetry,
the out-there is connected
     precisely
         to the over-here,
folded upon it
the ethics of poetry being that fold.

Listen: every day that I walk over-there,
near the crushed buildings
of North Philadelphia
downhill a glittering with turquoise glass
windshield smash cobbling in the low sun,
I see a minor junk heap caught in a gated foolery.[23]

All-Sport, twist-rib umbrella, small-car tire,
low combines, flat plastics, food box, baby rattle,
poptop, paper wad, and
an oak seedling,
can't help being pleased, that organic humanism,
it wasn't destined to last.

This out-there
in poetry is folded right over the right-here.
The stuff of this trash heap—
it is not empty thereness
but folds above, contains and envelops my nearness;

---

22. Lyons, 646.

23. "We can think of this deictic as meaning something like 'Look!' or
'There!' Such forms as Latin *ecce*, French *voici/ voilà*, etc. are worth not-
ing in this connexion: there function is quasi-referential, rather than
purely referential; and it is not always clear whether they are being used to
draw attention to an entity or to a place." (Lyons, 648) The slippage be-
tween entity and place is one that I feel offers a poetics or a sense of the
effect of the poetry I am writing.

the fold as ethical indistinction
between out-there and over-here
does not annul deixis, the
shaper/ sharper/ shepherd
of distinctions,
but articulates deixis as the fact of situations,
and traces the pull of mutual reference
that joins the there and here,
making deixis the process of the between.

I read something similar in theory of knots.

What happens if there is something that takes place that cannot be
pointed to
(like a massacre where all are gone, no evidence
        no one to acknowledge it
(like something glimmering on the edge of sensibility, shade of a
dream, twist of
        ineffable at the moment of its disappearance
(like something visible to which one mostly does not refer—big toe
transplanted to make
        a thumb, thalidomide surrealisms)

what is the status of the social agreement that something can be
pointed to,
what is the possible slippage between something that takes place and
something that is spoken of, what denials may block
"this inaugural act of reference"
from which "all other forms of reference will flow"[24]

call this the matrix of the unallowable, or, perhaps indifferently, say
loss

call this the problem of the dead

call it the toll

It is the space of poetry.

---

24. Godzich, "Foreword" to de Man, *The Resistance to Theory*, xvii.

Poetry seeps a little line, wayward, tumbles over the bumps around
the rocks, one did not think to call this weeping;
the rocks upon which we were sleeping;
inside the crack, leverage of detail
        imagines situations, not that they
                never did or never could
        for they did come from somewhere, but where?
Enormousness of universe, and enormity of what has happened
in our milky corner
of it, of it
"unraveling voice."

A sense of being
        a small seam split inside a little existence

yod, iota, jot, tittle and mote:

that is strange, simply strange,

        even allowing for laws of subtraction and physics.

"I'm sorry but
        from where you are
                I didn't quite catch your name."

                        October-December 1997; February–April 1998

Draft 34: Recto

O pocks of broken asphalt

let it go back to weed,
                    the driveway that paved the 50s
        killed at least one tree

        all of many colors
        lustrous

        scraps
        scrips

                of seedy beech and clusters
        of leaf balls

        of old oak drays
                pushed out from the tree
under a street light—there,

so—   refracting
                fragments of squirrel life
                of squirreled life
        tumble into the space behind the space?
                fraction
                fiction
  into pronouns?
                gather where the skittering gathers

having pillaged through "it"?
        having cited ecstasies "of" itness
bumbles "of" little objects
        thinning "of" crickets' pallid run-down whistle

in order to mark
with a yellow-yillow hi-lite

236

"un petit bit"
it in little, little in it.

That was a question
of what
I wanted to say—
"of"—
I am empty
this is true
there's no point to it.

To push thru the deep dream station
     and still miss the train,
to tear up the stairs for the dream el
     running ever
never to catch it
     the token—hard to tell from money—
hard to tell from memory
     stuck unfound.

By the time all this occurred
and the one in the booth had used up
infuriating
infiniating
time,
the train was
as they say in the blues
long
gone.

Stranded
by the empty track
I wanted to state flat things
without intervention
without invention—things
     of such evident rightness that
evidentiary witness
     with no retainer,

—That what?
Then what?
          What would have been achieved?
What, anyway, was outcome?

Meantime "bad memory,
no donut."
          But memorializing
isn't the issue.

Thereupon
comes everything I did not
          think once to
          say, but now shall say twice:
                    That the beyond
is now
          (*or not*)
                    in the surface

That the whole is strains "of"
          thinking what the whole and its fractions
                    come to

That it is—
and I've said only this—
a gloss on it
a gloss on is

glazed
          applied to ceramics
from rain.

And That there is a knife in the page
sometimes one can find it
given its addresses
its addressees

somewhere between recto and verso

in echt verses
found penetrating.

That memory
    is blunt dull knife.

That memory also is a knife,
    but blunt and dull

a thing one wants incisive, but
    instead puts flat red streaks

though sometimes it surprises
    and makes a ragged, fractal cut.

The whole is the knife that descends
and debate ensues
about the nature and kind
of the threat

but on the finger
that arrests it
changing the outcome
there is only one tiny spot
one pressure dot.

Now say that the whole
emerges from this
single interrupt,
that it is all
here,
angelic dot
<.>
the complete address

with it being the point
of
pointing in the first place

the zim of zum,
the zine of zaum.

Then say that this dot is really nothing.
Really is nothing.

All kinds hair
all kinds dust
all kinds dots—
Traces of something both present and absent
throwing a little knot of dust and hair
suspended
       to winds
in another time
       by chance,
              knot and knife
              knife and knot
thickness of breath and care—
       notwithstanding.

So what's more to say?
What's to say more?
Open the door.

In the maror phase
in apples
       in binding
in honey
       error
too much cinnamon
  got shook in,
      shock in
splash,
more than a dash,

so add more wine, more honey
more almonds, raisins
rozhenkes mit mandln
raisins with almonds

    cut in more apple
to point more "brick" (charoset)
    covenants.

Then a secret
(garam masala) to taste.
Add it.
All of it, point blank.

And afterwards,
    after words
        with the door shut,
should I let Elijah's winecup—
    a whole goblet, so hopeful—
just go to waste?
            Not a chance.

You can see at a glance
    how I take my place
in a lineup of unbelieving
    Jews who
took the cup   and drank.

May–November 1998

Draft 35: Verso

        Recto
        verso

      casting back return a void
      upon particular lines of word

    castings beck   *how*
  & squirmed thru   *vigorous scribbles*
      suggest

      break
         and null
            deep space.
    Turn the page
         maybe full.

Listen—
If there's any "Verse" here, it needs to be marked <vex>
    in the doggerel tradition; deprecatory puns on verse
        always claim to go from *bad* to *worse;*
    but Now we make new DocCode pacts
        individuating "verse extracts";

      Plausible (is it) still to talk about
      persistent saffron smell in a jar labeled poetry
      or myrrh in my pocket?
      —O pocks, or pox, of the detail
      saffron-colored room with skyblue far,
      deep-talki essence of book-star?
These facts of turning and re-turning: fold and X.

      Ebb and show
      Knife and knot
      Deictic dot

in the dim drawn day to which I woke

a half-worm, lucent pink in grey
stoppen in its track
sidling juice: vers
o worm towards verse

Turn the page.
A verso puts one page
upon the next
thickening the compost of the text

pages laid layer upon layer
doubling each other like rachel and leah.

Run them thru the X – – – x

done over & over   x upon x
the pages would drink in
black ink jet forces or heat – dark
copia
stretch

of the over-full cartridge's

STRETTO

everything spurts by entrance and overlap

a plague of logos black on black

thru perfect clarity into perfect opacity

strewing the

WORDS

pli upon pli   *he said*   *brightness* plea upon plea

and no one   *owns it*

a procedure

to produce from "moving masses whose
shape is unnameable"

some pile, some profile

a reminder of intricacy cross these works

that speaks in (and for) the convergence of quirks

while increasing the size of the background.

I open my little book
its pages are all white.

All right.

I haven't apparently   *written anything there yet.*

"I'm so not running down that road again"

I'm a complete stranger here
But You Are   *in this other language*

and You Did
straining
and You wander
roving, reversing, even revering
"the cold streets
of the revenants"
snot wipes, a shimmer of silver
on the already
cakey wristlet

Rusted stalled machinery

junked cars loaded with optionals
what's to know? the status quo

"starry lake of sky
with glowing arch of brilliance   *called itself it*
(or whatever)"

Everything is thrown away   *and said impossible*
and It's all still here   *Diaspora and destruction*
          passed by down the road
          passed down from road to road

waiting
          a ripped map in front of where I was.

          I saw Headlines readers
                    might tear off their Newspapers
          and paste them on the blank page
                    as a Method   "slice of truth"
                    in pre-packed words
          thin description it might be called,
                    shouldn't we embrace it?

"It was easier   I saw flickers
     in Nam   of lost substance
     to keep yr buddies   just like the odd word
                         to the side
                    "Derive"
'flat characters'"   and lurch out here

          For the little phrase
          half phatic, half erased
          the obverse
          that no one knows was said
          piping thru the dizzy channels
          of the night

          yet opens. Yes! it opens!

Lucky, that.

For people probably   can't be counted on

simply to
    "describe most thickly
        what matters most to them"

but let it leak

    when you and they

        look away

sometimes

    it can be found

at the turn of turning.

Does verso have and-yet another side
Not recto? The verso of verso.
Turns to where? Can it be read?
Is it here?

So even the loss is not "lost"?
    can I agree? And
        day of traversé
typical, am also skeptical
    I might mean "No."
Is it lost, or not?
Represented, or not?
In words, or without?
Present? And how?

Didn't I once say the reverse?

Have I mentioned all this as an argument for verse?

Drift she sd
    between the no and yes

derive (Fr.), derive (Eng.) draft
take your chances up front
it's nothing to be smug about
for one second you didn't
watch where you were going
and look what you got.
Therefore:

Au vers!
Need someone?
a pronominal volunteer

who "translates" *of*

arcs   stars   "stones"   wrecks   acts   strings   notes   dots

with a tetra-letter kit?   *and*
Unearthly
cascade of genitives

what cannot be named but
hangs
on unprimed canvas
like a comet
the text repeating bird-like
"come it"
aroused and ready-wet

Y *and* N *and* R *and* X

A million words   *all stet*
"I weep for you in all the letters of the alphabet"
a set of plants (some birds, some voles, etc.)
uncollected
song of songs, little scraps

dust

in the tunnels

of dust.

Which is why

every person has "their" shadow,
        why the ghost poem behind this ghost poem
has its existence,
            and why the dog's nose, the bat's map, the bird's zone
turn like a page
        and underneaths come up

            shadow things inside behind the said
        not light-space-time in the abstract (as the universe)
            the original awkward as its translation

the weave of a brown deco throw exactly the same on top and reverse

"overnourishing signs"   in particular   "overnourishing signs"

fat

GHOSTI

o this   o that

o

O!

Hence "She started naming things, places
        as she filled them up."

What a work!

And in a parallel way
        as she emptied them.

November 1998–February 1999

Draft 36: Cento

1/33   *Translation says the unsayable twice, once in another language.*

2   Take colloquial hypercorrection ("went with she and I")—

3   Min tedas liaj longaj rakontoj.

4/32   *It didn't work out now, did it?*

5   Not the right language; it was flat, unplanhed

6   had too many j's, pronounced "oy,"

7/31   *adding another edge to the page.*

8   It made for confusions of hope (esperanto) and Esperanto

9   of zaum and zimzum; and maybe this is, too.

10/30   "Self-valuable words"—samovity slova—*do not exist as such.*

11/30   *They can only be marked* as situated excess.

12   I mean, everything means something, somewhere.

13/29   *Like everyone else* I am attracted

14/29   *to words ending in -ette—*

15   like Rockette, majorette, poette,

16/28   *so strange in the language—*

17   O they make my heart go pitter-pat.

18   Kick, girls, in the face of it.

19/27 *It's the work of a moment*

20   in mitn derinnen

21   to fall into the emptiness of (real) words

22/26 *dazed amid the reall world the real real world*

23   and to wander outward there,

24   where kibbitzing debris doth me surround.

25/25 *Yet in effect it was*

26   something that happened daily,

27   a troth, a shma, to find wrds like that—it was prayer.

28/24 *Was there a choice? where was there?*

29/24 It happened. Emerged *into the lost and found of aphasia*

30   mezzo slova, wrong links, mish-moshed blocks

31/23 can't remember *where it is* and so

32/23 (*not in it at all*) I was here. But where was it

33   I wanted? Call this the lost and found of amnesia.

34/22 *Who heard the mixing of the tracks?*

35   Whirr wires inside. The wires knotted, surds

36   and could not note or knit the words

37/21 *that never were from anywhere, yet*

38/21 *formed place* and *formed changes.*

250

39   Did these words exist or not? Memories or not?

40/20   *Pause   space   work   space, inside emptiness*

41   inside the unsayable grumble hungry phonemes,

42   a space between, within, and deep aside my own.

43/19   So many prepositions, *so many ways to be lost.*

44   On paper (that is, this here), and what was here.

45   With paper folded so, so this (squeezed corpse, course exquis)

46/18   *gets to be another word, mote,* or mite, or mute.

47   The mote is mine

48   but I am also its.

49/17   *It's never what you think.*

50   That words, so filled with uses and compilations of meaning,

51   could also void themselves, streaming, and open themselves
        to loss.

52/16   *Who could credit*

53   the power of their insistence to present the remnants,

54   the erased of translation, theory of rubber smudges.

55/15   And so, like them, *I am drawing a blank*

56   over and over, and this crinkled, blotted blank

57   of being a foreigner in my language

58/14   *(a kind of scrying after all)*

59   makes its own non-native way between sayable and not.

60   Take this as poetics: Composition by Fold.

61/13 *Something definite, so to speak.*

62   The lucid utopia of Esperanto—

63   its hope that language does not follow power,

64/12 *this small evidence of hope, that our flawed light*

65   could make neutrality and syntactic ease

66   out of the sheer oddity of words—is done for, over.

67/11 *A shifting boundary that is strange*

68   remains. Another time throbs thru a membrane,

69   an original awkward as its translation

70/10 *readable in some parts, and sometimes in*

71/10 *other parts, or in the same parts, un-.*

72   This what we have.

73/9 *The space a presence possessed by other spaces.*

74   Words, babbling, make towers of allusion.

75   A single letter, black flake, blows back against the page.

76/8 *Sheens of A, luminosities of THE*

77   split and mingle at the sites of their articulation;

78   words empty and fill, empty and fill

79/7 *with spatter lines—what*

80   hope then for the wanderer?

81   The very hunger of hope.

82/6 That there's *always another little something*

83/6 *singes signaux cendre les plumes*

84   that will remain, even if said, unsaid.

85/5 *Trying to read what cannot be read*

86/5 *au bord du vide.*

87   Even no more sayings about anything, just

88/4 *the run thru the Bilingual*

89   the trek thru the Empty

90   the wandering thru the

91/3 *Unstatable: the what?*

92   This is where it began and where it begins

93   a dot glossing itself inside existence.

94/2 *Who cries? who listens?*

95   so keen to mark

96/2 *another   cry: whom; one of another, who?*

97/1 *Glistening thru those microtimes of day*

253

98/1   the fullwords lost, the lostwords full: *It is the*

99/1   *"It" characteristic of everything.*

October 1997

Draft 37: Praedelle

Hard. The dure of tradurre.
wide low arcdeep fields,
houses dotted, ho detto,
with shadow. And sun stark.

Stone and flesh, worry wort
no subtle word, true St. John's Wort.
Grab a bite at their Fat Lamb Inn.
Unstatable. The what?

Crumbling. "White plenitude"
Red boots, sea frets, wool smell
blanket wet with interior dew.
Close eyes. To See well.

Bring this from there,
this from here, that d'étrangère,
and something else, ormer,
gives long hoots from elsewhere.

One place cool and wide, second
hot and dry, third a salty isle.
With simple travelling steps — praedelle —
mix, shift and cambiare sides.

Assembling stagioni
stations and stages
shades of unspeakable iotas
seasons and ages.

Steep fell end becks
and calls to pasta — macaronic —
the "speech" of the sites,
in places tectonic.

Brough, pronounced Bruff
in the hard hills, on the scarp bares
Apt in two sites. Bones' slough.
Lark adds arc to aires.

Paglia e fieno
green and yellow tawdry
twine nests of edible color
hay listeth towards straw.

"High high high": name fits
phonemes diversi, threaded lects,
words org. in threes. Solve Riddles?
"Well, it's a fookin 'ill, ain't it"

Farfalle scamper and rise.
Kiting float. Stonewater jars
long peach lines of orrery
sunset orbitic law.

Bean of the sea-wall
chicken of the tree-well
lattice stripe language
high wind vowels

Chiaroscuro, and know why;
footnooted data, hypnic jerk
on the other side of verso
wads of salt grass lurk

Dream in the dream
of unspeakable Italian
cactus melon, due lingue
mixup round the homonym

Seameadow seagrass
pradera de Thalassia
She first thought watermelon
translated to acqua melone

Mite speaking.
Mote spoken.
Babble out the syllables
Présilly Hoboken.

Still-life with dishware
cooked earth meister-mixed
elbow on it, triple L.
attachments to fancy, nixed.

Dried lavender smells like tea.
Earl Grey and boxed milk
hot in a greenclad bowl.
Something definite so to speak.

Syntax built up
clarification matte;
mutes—cardboard, copper
black rubber and tin hat.

Dream sounds: was there somebody?
Dream thought: sentence about,
uh, language. Dream—damn.
No memory gets the sentence out.

Living alongside borders
A house called "Two Ways"
Rachel and Leah, why the choice?
in whose eyes?

Stand on the porch
between words and the speechless
as two female triangles
hug by pinkish arches.

Folds fall in laban-notation
from one to the other
striping the absolute
excitabilities of their billow.

They embrace and warm
shutters ope, windows wide
hearts terremoto pitter pat
pulse gold-white light.

In stucco corner where
four tonalities meet
they scatter origami foldits,
dream-awake or dream-asleep.

Wing-steep pitches folden valleys
ortolan quindi—
vantageless voice
of the brown feathery.

Postmemory l'altro ieri
or are there two or more
alongside that very where
darkened statue niches roar.

If one is saying yes, well then
t'other must say no.
Orphery, porphery.
There's just one way to go?

Win them; neither's a wrong one.
I love them both, even unseen
who'd eaten out of campo
the wild serrated green.

Dewy shadows of one caught
transfixed on the path
envelopments of instantaneous
black pitch, blank patch.

Name of the one for whom I named her
crepuscular twists of page
in éclairissage before a storm,
O range or rage.

Cooling down in grigio silence
Rime figures parlay soon.
The path (pith) coated with-white
by today-full moon.

Panned-in praedella, another quad
where moon and volcano
silver flames and gold. The ore, ecco,
that rifts claim.

Load eerie rift
with or, yes, what was he saying;
Keatskill to pack in smeltings
back to where they came from.

Rock gold into the open.
Stuff it into roll and rift
Impossible geology
of the gift.

Mined stuff into open earth.
Scrissi orto
verso ringaleaveo
recto on the straightaway, no dearth.

So I loaded the riffs
with terrific zaum
Itched thru the night
wandered the Raum.

Loaded them with either
then with or and both ("both both")
over the gravel rutted road
where "I" —they—walked.

Ciao Rachel, ciao Leah,
who brought to each the other.
Under keystone bridges found
Long-once dream of a double river.

The or of every rift is ore
the eithers also ores
There are twin rivers rushing wide
that flow apart to lodestar shores.

July 1998
Niccone Valley, Umbria

Draft 38: Georgics and Shadow

What did the work demand?
What did the work demand?

The knot.
That the question be asked.

Simply to go inside the fierce exactions of syntax and be answerable.
Shadows fall in every extension.

And detail. Time's rocks in space.
Ecliptic flaneuses.

The work exigent: "thought taking time."
Knot of string and rope and thread and leaves, all scales juncted, unravelable.

". . . wanting the tones and even the effect of its silences . . ."
The affect of its silences.

Tried to take soundings. No half measures. But the truth was—
The imagination of the ordinary is unimaginable.

The work gets woven from and knotted into its own shadow.
The work lies wrapt in its own shadow, cast back.

How did this work work?
So now what, now exactly what?

By knotted soundings. It said it all again.
There could be gestures; gets hard to avoid them.

Although what's done is done.
Insistence is a kind of elegy; the plumb a commonplace.

Wanted also social justice.
Does the elegiac sap, or motivate?

Nothing is inside the work, but everything is. The stillness of things not still.
To say is, is, is again and again, is very simple, very painful.

Absolute toll.
Every word teeming and bereft.

What are the tasks of the work?
Is time soluble inside (these) things?

The word means ergon — work, on the geo — land.
Work, despite insomnias of rage.

As a genre, the land of poetry.
Material time is linked to our softness, we fold over ourselves.

"I painted this cut branch by mixing ink in mist."
The exacerbation of the precious.

I sat in a room made of stone. Between the two, a third.
Such small stakes within the endless.

I wanted "a kind of mutedness" in words, silence without silencing.
Don't misunderstand if it is engraved in stone there on the "path of time."

The clots on the paper came from mixing ink with ash.
Could not decide between "it" and "is." So I left two midsized pebbles.

Cotto chipped at the lintel. Forget you'd ever said "center."
Untranslatable blots or shapes whose very blankness testified.

When did you finally know you would enter time by writing?
Around the razor wire ringlets wound plastic flags of ripped bags waving.

Saw thru, thought   then.
Saw of, might have been   if.

Is it Lyra in Vega or Vega in Lyra?
The clouds were curdled milk. My heart leap'd up at that.

How did you set to work?
Has any work gotten done?

I went roaring to the end of the runway.
Affirmation doesn't enter the absolute space.

Turned observation to observance.
Shared a self with the revenants.

Set out utensils: freshwater jar, and brushwater dip in the form of a furled leaf.
Way wide brown grey muddy.

Dreamed I set up darkroom in my mother's deep closet.
The monument was a chute.

Wanted social reverie, and then change. A fantasy.
"It" on the right side "is" on the left. A-moving, all a-moving.

Answering questions set by the dot, sited and forceful.
Chickadee, nuthatch, cardinal, junco, titmouse, house finch, and big mild doves.

What about any rock? OK, Rock.
Was the name Rilke, Rothko, Roethke?

In the work as rock can sometimes see roads of the world.
Was the phrase secret bliss, secret place, secret police?

Sometimes not.
Take it all as a loss.

And mistyped "throught."
Systole, diastole, evisceration, copia.

How did the work begin?
Was there a certain moment of identification?

Began 30 years late ago to set my own bees flying.
Salutations, teenage flowering pears, dark cypress, silvery olive, and squirrel-clipped tulips.

"I have a long history of starting."
Histories of startling.

The scratched crystal blurred the numbers. Perhaps it was right I lost my watch.
Salutations. The work is the horror of poetry as such.

Our names were missing from the title page of the book. Our work as if invisible, us shadowy, anonymous, unnamed. This was an irony only at the time.
Background of cancellations into which floats up the fad for acetate jackets, chartreuse, fuschia. Or a name: Vivian. A good little girl. DP. Post-war.

Tell loss. Telos. L is for Tally bone.
Tiniest skipper salamander. First person pile.

How does the work proceed?
What are the impulses for new work?

I make "choráls out of random input."
I make thin perambulations of loss.

Washed thru downsluice in gold and pink shine, I remain shadow.
A day inexplicably white with one goldfinch. The tongue of the bell.

Hearing the collusive chortle of collegial laughter.
Sent it snail mail, a response that rhymed.

Could experiment with a fan-shaped format. To toast your three-quarters skid and flashy slats of loss.
Eventail.

To time! L'chayim!
To Memory: "the thing I forget with."

But then I wanted to sing in Erse, an unknown-to-me northerly language, sing and sing in Erse.
Hey ho silly sheep.

Those old moon-gegenschein songs.
Tinted hallucinated cloth.

A set of poems, ancient Chinese, selected and translated from "the Nineteen Old Poems."
Whereas I feel the same way.

Yet when there is development, it seems banal; when there is aphorism, it seems incomplete. When there is tone, half-tones seem excluded.
Did it want gaps? Guesses only.

Make the whole work an Etruscan votive hearth—lustrous toy objects for serious placation.
Make a David Smith's "The Home of the Welder"—imbedding shards and symbols onto one plane, four walls. Little bronze house.

OK agree each work is the carcass of a cicada, green and silver-white oddity, a lost shell.
OK agree each work is a valise packed tight with allusions, a travelling kit.

Event. Taille.
Just a patch of volume there.

Claim nothing, then move on.
The underspeech is always diasporic.

What are the details?
How do you choose, or do you?

Swinging the bong of a bell inside memory makes a sound no one knew was hanging there, and which, when you listen for it, was the hallucination of poetry.
Parlons, parlong, parlone, parole.

Sweet flakes of time, amber insistence, and dropped daily, are called manna.
Letters scatter over the roads of earth.

Little gold dot on the glass that shines, is where everything is.
Cannot see for the deep dark, but the heaving shadows, bush and bliss.

Every letter is the inching of history, seen from so many miles, it is just what implacably happened and closer up, grief after grief, error after error, profit after profit, scarification and burning, the knife swung above the body. Initiation into what?
Wrestled all night. Gave way. No blessing.

Were there other bearings on the work?
And what other transfigurations of letters?

Holocause. And effect.
Doubles in unspeakable shadow.

Writing goes recto to verso, memory the other way. Poetry the wobbling pivot.
To orphanhood! Given these enormities, this has got to be our central tenet.

Sound. Hinge.
Wing of air.

Waves.
Assize.

Slowly the particulars scatter to the wind, starting with that shirt the color she used to say was "toy koise."
Do you still believe in the theory of the shard?

The word Unto.
Backbeat, hey ho.

"I make things because I want to."
Surface and beyond in one fold.

"They became little museums of the commonplace."
Coated with dilemma, bereft of story.

So resist "that ancient injustice toward the transitory."
So jump, mote, into the dancing whirl, despite powerlessness.

And work until it tolls.
And work until it tolls.

August 1998 – April 1999

Notes

〰〰〰〰〰〰〰〰〰〰〰〰〰〰〰〰〰〰〰

Draft 1: It. *Torn from (a page)* is the title of a painting by David Hannah; the section contains allusions to other of his paintings. The quip about "Rachel" is from a letter by Kathleen Fraser. There is also a buried statement by Paul Celan.

Draft 2: She. The artwork alluded to in the fifth section is Marcel Duchamp's *Etant Donnés*, an installation at the Philadelphia Museum of Art, and also the subject of my essay "Sub Rrosa" in *The Pink Guitar: Writing as Feminist Practice*. In this Draft there are also echoes of Gertrude Stein and H.D.

Draft 5: Gap. The deleted and blackened materials are intended to suggest the FBI files of George Oppen, which I received under the Freedom of Information Act when I was editing his *Selected Letters*. "The little child self" from Stephane Mallarmé's *The Tomb of Anatole*, specifically Paul Auster's translation. "An Activity . . ." is Regina Schwartz explaining interpretation; the notion of memory as interpretation in Mary Jacobus. "It is proper" from Luce Irigaray. The black books are by Anselm Kiefer. "Someone" is the dancer Sharon Friedler; "the form" occurs in Japanese music: *jo*—introduction; *ha*—the scattering; *kyu*—the rush to finish.

Draft 6: Midrush. The citation "Death is the moment . . ." from Annette B. Weiner, "Stability in Banana Leaves: Colonization and Women in Kiriwina, Trobriand Islands," in eds. Mona Etienne and Eleanor Leacock, *Women and Colonization: Anthropological Perspectives*, 287. "Rat-ta-tat-tat bébé" from Kurt Schwitters, UR-SONATA, 1923.

Draft 7: Me. Someone suggested that Emily Dickinson used the term "sky writing" in *Letters* I, 81–82, but she said writing by a "spirit pen on sheets from out the sky." An image of Remedios Varo's painting *Harmony* (1956) enters into one section.

Draft 8: The. "No continuing city," Hebrews 13:14. Description of "fours" from Trinity Day Care Center. Butterfly descriptions from *The Audubon Society Field Guide to North American Butterflies*, 819, 787, 795. "The work is work, however . . ." from James Scully's essay "Line Break," in

Line Break: Poetry as Social Practice. Jacob, in Genesis 32: 24–32. "What words . . ." from Margaret Holley's book on Marianne Moore.

Draft 9: Page. Horace, *Odes*: "I have constructed a monument more permanent than bronze and loftier than the noble Pyramids—a monument which no squalling rain, no gale-force winds can ever undermine. . . . In fact, I shall not totally die: a good chunk of me is going to escape funeral parlours." (My modification of a Penguin translation of III, xxx) "Making light" and "weaving webs" are H.D. on film; "tell the white marks" is William Carlos Williams on Marianne Moore, and "isolate flakes" alters Williams' *Spring and All*, poem xviii.

Draft X: Letters. "I have nothing to say . . .": modified from Walter Benjamin "N" from *The Arcades Project.* "Orphic hope . . ." Barbara Johnson. "Stickers, stamps . . ." Kurt Schwitters, or something about him. "More spindly . . ." Robert Hughes, *Time* (December 26, 1988). "The most poetical subject . . ." by E. A. Poe. "Je" etc., Arthur Rimbaud famously: "Je est un autre." "There is a company . . ." Beverly Blossom. "My spirit . . ." Robert Stepto. "Since we have already said . . ." Susan Horton. Gained tread on the smashing from Bradford Morrow's citing Dowell Coleman: "That compact little glass, a small wine glass—but broken it seemed to contain enough glass to make three, or four, that size."

Edmond Jabès (Rosmarie Waldrop, trans. *The Book of Shares*): "The readable is perhaps only the unreadable smashed to pieces."

Draft 11: Schwa. "The unsaid," M. M. Bakhtin, "Methodology for the Human Sciences." "Metamorphosis" and "petrified human desire" from Marianne Shapiro, *Hieroglyph of Time*. The line "Wer, wenn ich schrie," translated by me at several junctures from Rainer Maria Rilke, *The Duino Elegies*, I. "Gurnish helfin" is a Yiddish version of "gar nichts helfen."

Draft 12: Diasporas. "Creole of creoles," a phrase by Rei Terada. The end citation from Walter Benjamin, "Theses on the Philosophy of History."

Draft 13: Haibun. "Lethe" through "water . . .": modified from Leonard Kress, citing Pausanias. Lissajous figures: Philadelphia's Franklin Institute. Mayo Clinic letter cited by Marc Schogol in the Philadelphia *Inquirer*. "First patriotic": Sears ad. "Void-strewn": Maurice Blanchot on Mallarmé in *The Siren's Song: Selected Essays* (Bloomington: Indiana University Press, 1982). Readers interested in folk art may want to know that the Holstein's name is New Salem Sue.

Draft 14: Conjunctions. There are citations from the Philadelphia *Inquirer*, Metro section, Friday, April 6, 1990. There are citations from the Classification and Rating Administration (CARA) criteria for films. From an article by Meyer Shapiro, and an article by Paul de Man. The "social drained from his work" is a *New York Times* review (Sept. 8, 1989) of the photographs of Aaron Siskind.

"This point at which we see time as sizeless, involves us in infinity and is the point where 'here' coincides with 'nowhere.' To write is to discover this point." Maurice Blanchot, *The Sirens' Song: Selected Essays* 119.

Materials on Mass Observation, are, inter alia, from Humphrey Jennings and Charles Madge, "Poetic Description and Mass-Observation," *New Verse* 24 (Feb–March 1937); especially from David Chaney and Michael Pickering, "Authorship in Documentary: Sociology as an Art Form in Mass Observation," in *Documentary and the Mass Media*, ed. John Corner, London: Edward Arnold, 1986: 29–44. Also Diana Collecott, "H.D. and Mass Observation," *Line* 13 (1989); it is from this article that I first learned about Mass Observation.

"Fleshy" from an article by Linda Alcoff, in *Signs*. "Crossing, struggling, naming" is Geoffrey Hartman on Roland Barthes' analysis of Jacob and the Angel, in *Midrash and Literature*, ed. Geoffrey H. Hartman and Sanford Budick, New Haven: Yale University Press, 1986. "Watching doubting (etc.)" is Mallarmé's "Un Coup de Dés," as cited by Maurice Blanchot, *The Sirens' Song*, 245. "The size of the loss," Clayton Eshleman on exploration in poetry, *Conductors of the Pit,* New York: Paragon House, 1988, 5. "A certainty . . ." John Berger, on Picasso. Final words from Renée Block, "Midrash," in ed. Callaway & Greene, *Approaches to Ancient Judaism.*

Draft 16: Title. The ledger books with nipples by Dorothy Cross, from an installation called "Power House," Institute of Contemporary Art, Philadelphia, 1991, consisting in part of fourteen logbooks, cast wax, and steel bolts. "I am bourne . . .": Shelley's "Adonais." "Blurred and breathless," citation from *The Odyssey*, Book Eleven as translated by Robert Fitzgerald. Muthoplokon: the word by Sappho. The translation "myth plucker" from a poem of Ben Friedlander helped me on the way.

Draft 17: Unnamed. The citation from Bakhtin ("poetry depersonalizes 'days' . . .") is from "Discourse in the Novel," *The Dialogic Imagination*, 291. The line about "facts" is Michel Leiris, *Manhood*. The long citation, slightly modified from a news article headlined "Lithuanians Haunted by Holocaust," was written by *Philadelphia Inquirer* staff writer Fen Montaigne, and appeared July 27, 1992, on the front page. "Reasons to wonder," by Robert Storr, from DISlocations, a show at the Museum of Modern Art, New York, October 1991–January 1992. Memories of Rilke's *Duino Elegies* persist, here the ninth.

Draft 18: Traduction. This poem arose from four of the Drafts being translated into French at the Fondation Royaumont in October 1992, by a group of French poets and writers including Emmanuel Hocquard, Yves di Manno, Jean-Paul Auxeméry, Joseph Guglielmi, Françoise de Larocque, and Joey Simas, as well as Marcel Cohen, Esther Tellerman, and others. The first line was "given" by M. M. Antoine Ségovia and Philippe Mairesse (in a special envelope also at Royaumont) to provoke any one realization of the(ir) conceptual art piece "par le Menu" "oeuvre dont les acquisitions et les présentations successives *modifient* la forme." The line "face aux grands enjeux du siècle" is from a review by Yves di Manno of Eliot Weinberger. Fragments as "conspicuous oracles" is Philippe Sollers on Mallarmé. "More unstructured, wicked problems" is a citation from John Nosek of Temple University's Computer and Information Sciences. Some of the "nomadic occupation" sentence is by Robert Storr, speaking of the artist David Hammons, from the show called DISlocations. With thanks to Micheline Rice-Maximin, Serge Gavronsky, and J-P Auxeméry for checking (or signing off on) my French.

Draft 19: Working Conditions. "The traces of each successive handwriting regularly effaced as had been imagined have in the inverse order been (regularly) called back." Thomas de Quincey, "Suspira de Profundis." "Virile piety" is a phrase by Charles Derr, poet. Quotations about music are either by pianist John MacKay, program notes for Luciano Berio and Yusef Lateef, or from program notes on Joan La Barbara's vocal performances. "so I had a feeling tonight that nothing . . ." are three lines from David Antin's "scenario for a beginning meditation," in his *Selected Poems: 1963–1973,* Los Angeles: Sun & Moon Press, 144. "Not boiling to put pen to paper/ Perhaps a few things to remember—" is Louis Zukofsky, *"A"* 1 *"A,"* Berkeley: University of California Press, 1978, 4. "During my long nights . . .": said by V.Y. Mudimbe, African philosopher and poet, about fratricidal conflict in Rwanda in 1961, and quoted from the *PEN Newsletter* 81, Writers and Human Rights in Africa, (May 1993), 4.

Draft 20: Incipit. The material in italics draws on, but alters, lines of "First Dedication" in Anna Akhmatova's "Poem Without a Hero," *The Complete Poems of Anna Ahkmatova,* translated by Judith Hemschemeyer, Boston: Zephyr Press, 1992, 545. This Draft is the beginning of the first fold; it corresponds to Draft 1: It.

Draft 21: Cardinals. "But with Schönberg, affability ceases." (Adorno,

Prisms, 150). "Ghost pieces," come, as in Draft 19, from program notes for "Jacob's Room" by Morton Subotnick. "Studded with acquisitions . . . and layoffs." (Bruce Barber, The New Museum, brochure.) "On Foot I Made My Way Through the Solar Systems" is a short poem by the Swedish-language, Finnish poet Edith Södergran; I have cited the first three lines in modified form and extended the poem. The text is from Södergran's *We Women*, translated and introduced by Samuel Charters, San Francisco, Oyez Press, 1977. "A disorder of memory" echoes a title by Freud. The "encyclopedia" citation comes from my *Writing Beyond the Ending*, 102. Continuing the fold, this Draft corresponds to Draft 2: She.

Draft 22: Philadelphia Wireman. "The Philadelphia Wireman sculptures were found abandoned on a side street in Philadelphia on a trash night in 1982. . . . The entire collection totals approximately six hundred pieces and appears to be the creation of one person." It is surmised that the person is dead, because the objects were thrown out en masse. It is surmised that he was strong (i.e. male) because the thick wires seem to have been twisted without the help of pliers or other tools. And it is surmised that he was African-American because of the particular Philadelphia neighborhood in which they were found and because of the tradition of Kongo power objects on which these works seem to draw. The summary from Janet Fleisher Gallery, Philadelphia was written by John Ollman. "Traumscrapt" material from Linda Kauffman, *Special Delivery*. "Cursive scrimmage" from Alan Shima's description of Beverly Dahlen's work in *Skirting the Subject*, 129. Some descriptors throughout from Ann Jarmusch's reviews and stories of the Wireman's works in *ART News* and *The Philadelphia Inquirer*. Other descriptors, and list of items or objects used for the multimedia works by the Wireman from Janet Fleisher Gallery. All these descriptors and lists have been broken up and augmented. For the tradition of nikisi (pl. minkisi), the instruction to "randomize the flow of paths," and the question (actually applicable to a Kongo tomb tradition) "Can you tie up the anger of the dead?" see Robert Farris Thompson, *Flash of the Spirit: African and Afro-American Art and Philosophy*, 222 and 134. This Draft corresponds to Draft 3: Of.

Draft 23: Findings. I was reminded of ways of organizing time in Eviatar Zerubavel, *The Seven-day Circle: The History and Meaning of the Week*. Lee in section three is Lee Hickman, the much-mourned editor of *Temblor*. Evocation of the "Angel or the Power" is from H.D., *Sagesse*. "Oh baby" is a line from the Big Bopper's song, "Chantilly Lace." "Wet rails and the oil of crushed leaves" is SEPTA's explanation for late trains in autumn. The cricket paraphernalia at the Nelson Atkins Art Museum in Kansas City, Missouri. The "wee keeps" in section 17 by Bill Walton, Institute of Contemporary Art exhibit called "Conversation Pieces," June 1994, Philadelphia. Words in the last section are from William Carlos Williams, "January Morning." The reader might already have surmised that each section of this poem both enacts an hour of the day and also refers or alludes to the prior Draft corresponding to its particular number. The Draft also corresponds to Draft 4: In. "Findings" is thus doubly folded.

Draft 24: Gap. The citation from Walter Benjamin, "Theses on the Philosophy of History" (as at the end of Draft 12: Diasporas) and the girder—objectivist talisman—from Charles Reznikoff (*Jerusalem the Golden*) and George Oppen. There are also unmarked words from Garrett Stewart, Hank Lazer, Colleen Lamos, Victoria Harrison, and Uwe Kraemer. I also use, with thanks, a 1994 review of *Drafts*, in which Caroline Bergvall gave, as my phrase, "historical dead" instead of "historical dread." Thereupon I include a number of intentional typographical errors in this work, whose title is the same as Draft 5: Gap.

Draft 25: Segno. The doubled rocks were inspired by (but don't develop quite the same as) the work of Vija Celmins called *To Fix the Image in Memory* (1977–1982), consisting of eleven different real rocks set next to their uncannily identical replicas made by Celmins of painted cast bronze (Institute of Contemporary Art, Philadelphia). "Squandered" from Ingeborg Bachmann: "Or could he [Wittgenstein] mean that we've squandered our language because it contains no word that can touch upon what cannot be spoken?" *Songs in Flight: The Collected Poems of Ingeborg Bachmann,* trans. Peter Filkins, xxi. Girder/rubble, as before: Reznikoff/Oppen. Related to Draft 6: Midrush.

Draft 26: M-m-ry. The poet Rachel Tzvia Back was once my student. "The earth's inward, narrow, crooked lanes" comes from John Donne, "The Triple Foole." "The real world . . ." is Carl Rakosi. "We have reviewed the document," and so forth, in italics: a letter from that governmental body overseeing the administration of the Freedom of Information Act. Related to Draft 7: Me.

Draft 27: Athwart. "Conaissance inutile" is Charlotte Delbo's phrase about knowledge gained in, and by virtue of, the Holocaust. "Ragge of verses" is John Donne. "Useless scrap its power" is Eliot Weinberger on Cecilia Vicuña. The citation about the artist is from a *Times* review of Aaron Siskind (as in Draft 14). Related to Draft 8: The.

Draft 28: Facing Pages. "Intransitive verbs": the writer Charles Bechtel. "Powerful little berries": First Nations people about the glass beads of Venice traded to them. "Showbread": Exodus 25: 30. "Circumstances of its composition . . . disturbances of the poet" and subsequent phrases (modified): from Peter Quartermain, a paper on Robert Duncan. "Cold ashes": Ingeborg Bachmann, as in Draft 25. The donor draft is Draft 9: Page.

Draft 29: Intellectual Autobiography. I had been composing Drafts for ten years, for they began in early 1985; Draft 29, harkening also to Draft X: Letters, was written as an anniversary work. The list of genres from Scaliger, *Poetices*, 1617, cited by O. B. Hardison. Grant application language cribbed from the usual suspects. "Baffled . . ." is a self-citation from 1985, one of the initiatory recognitions. Dora Maar's 1936 photograph, along with Lisa Liebmann's citation (p. 126) about Yves Klein in Bice Curiger, *Meret Oppenheim*. "*Compelling any writing*": Louis Zukofsky, "Mantis: An Interpretation," *ALL the Collected Short Poems, 1923–1958*, New York: W. W. Norton, 1965, 75. "Work": George Oppen—an incident appropriated from a friend. The citation about "household" art is slightly altered from Faith Wilding, "Monstrous Domesticity," M/E/A/N/I/N/G 18, p. 7. The saxophone—a description of the childhood of LaMonte Young, based on *The Philadelphia Inquirer*, November 28, 1995, F4. Some of the forms of paper that Emily Dickinson used, described by Mabel Todd Bingham in *Bolts of Melody*, xii–xiv. Nicht mitmachen—an ethics of resistance in Theodor Adorno, from whom also the mote as strabismic lens and the challenge to post-Holocaust poetries, "nach Auschwitz . . .": "After Auschwitz, to write a poem is barbaric," from *Prisms*. "That we are inconsolable," from Nicolas Abraham and Maria Torok, *The Shell and the Kernel: Renewals of Psychoanalysis*, p. 130. "Raining songbirds" is from David Hankla, a field supervisor for the U. S. Fish and Wildlife Services, in a news article, November 27, 1995, *The Philadelphia Inquirer*, A4.

Draft XXX: Fosse. The little book does, in fact, exist. It is by Ann Hamilton, in a private collection. Included are muted, unmarked, or vaguely signaled citations from Louis Zukofsky, Armand Schwerner, *Beowulf*, Donald Rackin, Ezra Pound, and John Felstiner on the Paul Celan/ Nelly Sachs correspondence. See Draft 11: Schwa.

Draft 31: Serving Writ. "common air . . .," Zukofsky, "A"–6, "*A,*" 26 –27; "another edge . . .," Rod Smith; "disquieting . . .," Luce Irigaray; "gold sweat," Barbara Guest. See Draft 12: Disasporas.

Draft 32: Renga. Among other sources, some undergraduate students saying particular things, mainly about Lyn Hejinian—Tiambe Belardo (section 27), Holly Bittner (section 45), Carol Ann Gross (section 86), Stephanie Smith (section 49). Section 3: poet Michael O'Brien. Section 4: the basket maker and sculptor is Dorothy Gill Barnes. Section 5: sideshadows as a concept—Gary Saul Morson and Michael André Bernstein. Section 8: Kathleen Fraser on my poem "Writing"; also Psalm 102. Section 15: paraphrased from Johanna Drucker, reviewing Julie Cohn. 26 comes from Sue Wells out of Plato. 30—"little i" comes from somewhere I can't now remember. Section 40: Margaret Cavandish, as cited by Denise Riley, "*Am I That Name.*" Section 44: Jacques Derrida. Section 49, "the site of watchfulness" is Kathleen Fraser on the line. Section 51: Ann Yearsley. Section 52: "unassuaged unrest": Theodor Adorno in *Negative Dialectics*, 203. Section 58: Cid Corman's translation of Basho, *Back Roads to Far Towns*, 81. Section 60: Keats, *Endymion*, Book I. Section 67: cited from Ann Snitow. Section 68: said by Rudolf Steffel, potter. Section 77 is about one of Daniel Goode's clarinet compositions. Section 93: *Columbia University Alumni Magazine* citing Xiaodong Song. Section 95: Sherwood Anderson. Draft 13: Haibun is the fold.

Draft 33: Deixis has footnotes that may be consulted for references. Professor Muffy Siegel helped when I was well into this draft with some discussion of deixis in linguistics; she is not responsible for any flaws in presentation here. I offer thanks to Pattie McCarthy for an unmarked citation, to Lawrence Venuti for the translator's visibility, and to Gregg Biglieri for some bibliography.

Draft 34: Recto. "Un petit bit," French novelist and sociologist Azouz Begag, in conversation. N.B. the bumper sticker is Bad Cop, No Donut. "Rozhenkes mit mandln," an apparently folk lullaby in Yiddish, in fact composed by Mark Warshawsky. Draft 15: Little is the fold.

Draft 35: Verso. Coding <vex> is DocuComp for verse extract. Myrrh, from H.D. "Deep-talki," from Melvin B. Tolson. Moving masses, from Arnold Schoenberg (cited by Clark Coolidge). "I'm so not . . ." Kaz Haviland and Koré DuPlessis, after seeing a *vipere*. "Starry lake" from student Mike Weiss. "I weep" is modified from Chaim Grade (translated from the Yiddish by Cynthia Ozick). Wrote some Jerry Rothenberg, listening to his narrative. "Flat characters" from student and veteran Barry Grossman. Critique of "thick description"—Renato Rosaldo. "Overnourishing signs" is Roland Barthes. The other worker is Grandma (Tressa) Prisbey of Simi Valley, California—from "The Story of Bottle Village" by Verni Greenfield. Related to Draft 16: Title.

Draft 36: Cento. Cento is a "patchwork"—a poem in which every line is cited, often from epics. This is a partial cento, built of 99 lines—and that, for its simple allusion to the wrong word, "cent," or one hundred. Here at least every third line is cited, "borrowed" from my own long poem. The re-cited lines in Draft 36: Cento occur in order, but they reverse the order of their appearance in the poem to date. The first line here is from Draft 33: Deixis (being written as I composed this work). The fourth line is from Draft 32: Renga, the seventh from Draft 31: Serving Writ, and so on back to the final lines, from Draft 1: It. The main donor draft is Draft 17: Unnamed.

The Esperanto translates into "his long stories bore me." Planh is the Provençal word for lament. Zimzum (tsimtsum) is contraction, the world defined by God's withdrawl, and the point—or vacuum, that is left. Samovity slova, or "self-valuable words" apparently from the Russian of Roman Jakobson: a definition of zaum. The Yiddish "in mitn derinnen" means all of a sudden. Shma is Hebrew for "Hear," the beginning of a daily prayer. Mezzo means middle or half in Italian. I also cite from the French translation of Draft 6: Midrush and Draft 5: Gap (Faille, in the French title), accomplished by J-P Auxeméry and the Royaumont collective. "Singes signaux cendre les plumes" translates "marked/ markers ash the foiled/ feathers" while "Au bord du vide" translates "Right on the edge."

Draft 37: Praedelle. "'Load every rift' of your subject with ore." John Keats letter to P. B. Shelley, 1820. "Both/ both" is Anne Waldman, from *Jovis* I.

Draft 38: Georgics and Shadow. "Thought taking time" (Peter Middleton); "the effect of its silences . . ." (Charles Altieri, both in *The Objectivist Nexus*). "Mixing ink in mist" (Kim Ung-Won, Korean artist, 1913). "Mutedness" paraphrased from W. G. Sebald. The monument—to Walter Benjamin, courtesy of photos by Beth Scroggin. "History of starting" (Charles Derr). "Chorál out/ of random input" (Zukofsky, "A" 14, "*A*," 354, plural without his linebreak). "Of loss" (from Charles Bernstein on Charles Reznikoff, *Objectivist Nexus*). "Thing I forget with" (Douglas Crimp, citing Roget's *Thesaurus*?). "Silly sheep" from Edmund Spenser. "Tinted hallucinated cloth" (Elaine deKooning on Mark Rothko). Chinese poems, from *The Penguin Book of Chinese Poetry*. David Smith at the Tate Gallery, London. Duchamp at the Philadelphia Museum of Art. Enormities, passim; in March–April 1999, the creation of refugees in Kosovo. "Because I want to" (Wesley Tanner bookmaker @ Naropa, 1998). "Museums of the commonplace" (Esther McCoy, *Naives and Visionaries*). "Injustice toward the transitory." (Adorno, his essay on the essay). The donor draft is Draft 19: Working Conditions. This completes the first two units of Drafts—the first works, and the first fold.

Rachel Blau DuPlessis is Professor of English and Creative Writing at Temple University and author of six books of poetry: *Wells* (Montemora, 1980), *Tabula Rosa* (Potes & Poets, 1987), *Draft X: Letters* (Singing Horse Press, 1991), *Drafts 3–14* (Potes & Poets, 1991), *Drafts 15–XXX. The Fold* (Potes & Poets, 1997), and *Renga: Draft 32* (BeautifulSwimmer, 1998). She has also published four critical books, including *The Pink Guitar: Writing as Feminist Practice* (Routledge, 1990), and *Genders, Races and Religious Cultures in Modern American Poetry, 1908–1934* (Cambridge University Press, 2001). She is the editor of *The Selected Letters of George Oppen* (Duke University Press, 1990). Her poems and essays have appeared in numerous journals and anthologies.